# How to use your Snap Revision Text Guide

This *Coram Boy* Snap Revision Text Guide will help you get a top mark in your Edexcel English Literature exam. It is divided into two-page topics so that you can easily find help for the bits you find tricky. This book covers everything you will need to know for the exam:

**Plot:** what happens in the novel?

**Setting and Context:** what periods, places, events and attitudes are relevant to understanding the novel?

**Characters:** who are the main characters, how are they presented, and how do they change?

**Themes:** what ideas does the author explore in the novel, and how are they shown?

**The Exam:** what kinds of question will come up in your exam, and how can you get top marks?

To help you get ready for your exam, each two-page topic includes the following:

## Key Quotations to Learn
Short quotations to memorise that will allow you to analyse in the exam and boost your grade.

## Summary
A recap of the most important points covered in the topic.

## Sample Analysis
An example of the kind of analysis that the examiner will be looking for.

## Quick Test
A quick-fire test to check you can remember the main points from the topic.

## Exam Practice
A short writing task so you can practise applying what you've covered in the topic.

## Glossary
A handy list of words you will find useful when revising *Coram Boy* with easy-to-understand definitions.

**AUTHOR:**
**STEVE EDDY**

**ebook**

To access the ebook v
Snap Revision Text Gu

collins.co.uk/~~~~~~~

and follow the step-by-step instructions.

Published by Collins
An imprint of HarperCollins*Publishers* Ltd
1 London Bridge Street
London SE1 9GF

HarperCollins*Publishers*
1st Floor, Watermarque Building
Ringsend Road
Dublin 4, Ireland

© HarperCollins*Publishers* Limited 2021

ISBN 978-0-00-847178-1

First published 2021

10 9 8 7 6 5 4 3 2 1

British Library Cataloguing in Publication Data.

A CIP record of this book is available from the
British Library.

Commissioning: Katie Sergeant and
    Richard Toms
Author: Steve Eddy
Editorial: Frances Cooper
Reviewer: Jo Kemp
Cover Design: Sarah Duxbury
Inside Concept Design: Ian Wrigley
Typesetting and artwork: Q2A Media
Production: Karen Nulty

With thanks to Jamila Gavin for all her
support, insights and additional material.

Printed in Great Britain by Martins the Printers

ACKNOWLEDGEMENTS
The author and publisher are grateful to
the copyright holders for permission to use
quoted materials and images.
Every effort has been made to trace copyright
holders and obtain their permission for the
use of copyright material. The author and
publisher will gladly receive information
enabling them to rectify any error or omission
in subsequent editions. All facts are correct at
time of going to press.

All quotations from *Coram Boy* are
reproduced with kind permission of David
Higham Associates.

# Contents

# Prologue and Chapters 1 to 4

**You must be able to:** understand how Gavin introduces characters, themes and settings in the Prologue and first four chapters.

## How does the Prologue suggest themes?

A 'fine lady' is told by a gypsy she will have seven babies. When this prediction proves true, the lady asks the midwife to drown six of them, but their father saves them. On their seventh birthday, the six reappear and the lady dies of shock. This introduces the themes of **fate**, abandoned children, children saved by kindness and the price paid for deception.

## How are Otis Gardiner and his son Meshak introduced?

The first three chapters introduce the unscrupulous Otis Gardiner and his unworldly and vulnerable 14-year-old son Meshak. Otis regards Meshak as a curse, and often uses his whip on him. He is a cruel but charming man, and good at pretending to be caring. He makes a living as a pedlar, travelling as far as Gloucester and London. It is gradually revealed that he also gets paid to take unwanted children and then sells them to the navy or army, or to provide cheap labour. Worse, he accepts money to ensure that **illegitimate** babies are looked after, and then buries them in ditches – sometimes still alive. Meshak hates having to help him.

Meshak is excited when their wagon arrives in Gloucester. Here Otis womanises and drinks in the Black Dog inn, and discusses immoral money-making schemes with the landlady, Mrs Peebles. He also bumps into Mrs Lynch, who 'flirtatiously' invites him to visit Ashbrook.

In Chapter 3, when 'the brats' are disposed of, Meshak has time to go to the cathedral, where he loves to look at stained-glass saints and angels. He regards one angel as his own, and sometimes she 'takes' him to 'see' his dead mother.

## How are Thomas and Alexander introduced?

In Chapter 4, Otis's corrupt world is contrasted with that of Gloucester Cathedral's choir school and two choirboys who become loyal friends: Alexander Ashbrook, from a wealthy **aristocratic** family, and Thomas Ledbury, son of a ship's carpenter.

As a new boy at the school, Thomas is tormented by other boys until Alexander tells him that this will stop if Thomas can make them laugh. This works and Thomas becomes very popular.

Both boys are musical, but whereas Thomas is light-hearted and amusing, Alexander is usually serious, and is deeply devoted to music. When Thomas goes to spend August with Alexander's family, he at first wonders how he will fit in, but he becomes popular there too, though Mrs Milcote is disdainful towards him.

On the way to Ashbrook, Alexander and Thomas encounter Otis and Meshak, which links their two worlds and hints at the danger presented by Otis.

## Key Quotations to Learn

'Oi! Meshak! Wake up, you lazy dolt!' (Otis: Chapter 1)

'You are my angel. I would die for you.' (Meshak: Chapter 3)

[Alexander has] a dazed, inverted look, as if he lived more inside himself than outside. (Chapter 4)

## Summary

- Otis is charming, but also cruel, ambitious and unscrupulous. He makes money from selling children, and by falsely promising desperate women that he will make sure their babies are cared for. He then blackmails them.

- Meshak quietly tolerates mistreatment by Otis. People think Meshak is empty-headed, but he sees an inner spirit world.

- Otis and Meshak cross the River Severn and arrive in Gloucester. Otis visits Mrs Peebles in the Black Dog; Meshak visits 'his' stained-glass angel.

- Thomas is bullied at the choir school until Alexander tells him how to stop it by employing his natural ability to entertain.

- Alexander is a gifted musician. He and Thomas become friends, and Thomas goes to stay at Ashbrook House.

## Questions

QUICK TEST
1. What does Otis usually do with the babies he is given?
2. Why does Meshak love the cathedral?
3. Which member of the Ashbrook household does Otis meet at the Black Dog?
4. How does Thomas stop getting bullied?
5. How does Mrs Milcote treat Thomas when they are introduced?

EXAM PRACTICE
Write a paragraph analysing the relationship between Otis and Meshak at this point.

# Chapters 5 to 9

**You must be able to:** understand how Gavin introduces characters and their lives at Ashbrook.

## How does Chapter 5 develop the characters of Thomas, Melissa and Mrs Milcote?

Sensitive and observant, Thomas senses the 'sneering laughter' of the servants at his expense. However, the assistant housekeeper, Mrs Morris, kindly offers to tell him what to wear.

Things further improve for him when he entertains all the children in the nursery. However, the party is broken up by the disapproving Mrs Milcote.

Mrs Lynch eavesdrops on Melissa complaining to her mother, and concludes that Mrs Milcote hopes Melissa will marry Alexander.

## What do we learn about Lady Ashbrook in Chapter 6?

Lady Ashbrook has tried to keep the peace between Alexander and 'his stern and conscientious father', who wants him to give up music. She now reluctantly agrees with her husband.

The story shifts to Ashbrook's orphanage. Lady Ashbrook is sympathetic to the plight of poor, unmarried mothers and their children, but Admiral Bailey and Mrs Ridley think they should turn away more mothers, and feel that improving conditions will encourage illegitimacy. We learn that Lady Ashbrook was shocked by how badly run the **parish** orphanage was. Her husband was 'outraged' that she wanted to help, but she persuaded him: she is 'a headstrong woman as well as persuasive'. She had the slovenly parish nurse replaced, and now works to improve conditions.

## What happens in the cottage in the woods?

In Chapter 7, Thomas falls off a horse, and Alexander takes him to Waterside, Ashbrook's 'little play cottage' to recover. Isobel and Melissa are there, along with Alexander's younger siblings Alice and Edward. All are delighted to see Thomas and make him continue his story of Dawdley Dan. Meshak, however, secretly spying on the happy scene, is amazed to see what he thinks is 'his' angel from the cathedral – Melissa. He vows to be her protector.

## How does Alexander's life change in Chapters 8 and 9?

Lady Ashbrook praises Thomas for 'turning [Alexander] into a human being'. Thomas has 'never felt happier'. After supper, the young people provide musical entertainment. We learn how torn Lady Ashbrook now feels between her husband's insistence that Alexander must give up music, and Alexander's that music is his life. When he sings 'The Silver Swan', she is transfixed, but the mood is darkened by sarcastic slow clapping from Sir William Ashbrook, who thinks music is 'for the serving classes'.

In a windy, moonlit **Gothic** setting, Thomas is 'filled with unease' when he glimpses Meshak spying on Melissa.

Ashbrook prepares for a ball. The lavish spread of food contrasts with the conditions of the starving poor. Meshak hangs around trying to glimpse 'his angel' Melissa.

The worlds of Otis and Ashbrook are brought closer together when Mrs Lynch uses argument and flirtation to persuade Otis that they can earn money from her local knowledge. It is implied that Mr Claymore, the magistrate, has got his teenage **ward** pregnant and that they have handed the baby over to Mrs Peebles.

When Meshak sees Alexander and Melissa kissing, his howl of anguish sounds to them like 'all the demons of hell'.

## Key Quotations to Learn

How he wished he had never come. (Thomas at Ashbrook: Chapter 5)

From now on, he would be her guardian and protector. (Meshak on Melissa: Chapter 7)

Thomas, so natural and unassuming, so funny and kind, made him see the world in a gentler light. (Alexander: Chapter 8)

## Summary

- Thomas feels awkward at Ashbrook, but soon feels accepted.
- Lady Ashbrook wants to improve the orphanage.
- Thomas continues to entertain in the play cottage.
- Sir William wants Alexander to give up music.
- Mrs Lynch persuades Otis to do business with her.
- Meshak sees Alexander and Melissa kissing.

## Questions

QUICK TEST
1. How is Mrs Morris kind to Thomas?
2. How does Admiral Bailey disagree with Lady Ashbrook?
3. Where is Melissa when Meshak first sees her?
4. Who wants to do business with Otis?
5. Why does Meshak howl?

EXAM PRACTICE
Write a paragraph explaining what sources of conflict and potential difficulty arise in this section.

# Chapters 10 to 14

You must be able to: analyse events leading up to Alexander leaving Ashbrook.

## How does Chapter 10 portray the relationship between Isobel and Melissa?

Isobel feels that Melissa is taking her place as Alexander's closest friend. Melissa reassures her and explains that she has started her periods.

At the play cottage, events to come are **foreshadowed** by Alice and Eddie playing 'mothers and fathers' with a doll. In another Gothic scene, Alice is frightened by Meshak 'peeping' at them. Nanny frightens him off.

## What does Chapter 11 reveal about Otis and the Coram Hospital?

Mothers trust Otis with their babies. Meshak is used to hearing these 'weeping, pathetic voices', and to dumping their babies. In London, they visit Coram, and we hear of its lottery admission system. Otis takes the babies of wealthy mothers to the back door, where chief nurse Sarah Wood sneaks them in.

Meshak goes to a graveyard to 'talk to his angels'. **Ironically**, a gravedigger moves him on: 'Get out of here, you heathen idiot. ... Don't you know this is hallowed ground?'

Otis and Meshak go to London Docks to sell four Coram boys. As Otis is negotiating, some slaves come ashore. Otis agrees to take one African woman's baby for the four boys. He knows there is 'money in black infant boys'.

## How and why does Alexander leave home for good?

In Chapter 12 the Ashbrook family attend a Christmas concert, only to find that Alexander cannot sing because his voice has broken. Sir William seizes on this as his cue to take Alexander away from the choir school. Back at Ashbrook, Alexander is furious to find his father has banned musical instruments. When Alexander complains, his father beats him.

The mood in the house is one of 'tension and suppressed anger', preparing the reader for an explosion. Alexander's only relief from estate management is when Melissa visits his bedroom. He embraces her, and she tells him that he can play the **virginals** at Waterside.

Alexander decides to leave Ashbrook. He writes a letter to his father explaining this, and another to Melissa, which he takes to Waterside. While he is playing a **tragic** piece of music there, Melissa arrives, they make love, and then part.

## What happens after Alexander leaves Ashbrook?

Sir William angrily disinherits Alexander. Isobel blames Melissa for him leaving. Melissa is horrified to find, from Tabitha, that she is pregnant. She goes to a pond to drown herself, but a reflection in the water (Meshak's) changes her mind. She confides in Isobel and the pair are reconciled and fantasise about bringing up the baby.

Mrs Lynch guesses that Melissa is pregnant and begins to scheme.

Chapter 14 begins with Meshak's vision of dead babies in a tree. He goes to Waterside – the play cottage – and is frantic when he hears Melissa scream in childbirth.

Mrs Milcote trusts Mrs Lynch, who says they must tell Melissa the baby is dead, and she will give it to 'the Coram man' so that Melissa can make a fresh start. Otis gives the baby to Meshak to get rid of, but Meshak resolves to take it to Coram. This ends Part 1.

## Key Quotations to Learn

The land must be cared for as you care for it. But I am not the man to do the job. (Alexander letter to Sir William: Chapter 12)

'You've ruined our lives.' (Isobel to Melissa: Chapter 13)

Mrs Lynch's voice coiled as slithery smooth as a serpent, but to poor Mrs Milcote it sounded like honey. (Chapter 14)

## Summary

- Melissa has her first period.
- Otis trades four boys for a black baby.
- Alexander's voice breaks: he must leave the choir school.
- Sir William bans music, and beats Alexander, who resolves to leave Ashbrook. Before he does, he and Melissa make love.
- Melissa becomes pregnant and Mrs Lynch arranges for Otis to take her baby. Meshak takes it to Coram.

## Questions

QUICK TEST
1. What is the significance of Alice and Eddie playing 'mothers and fathers'?
2. What event makes Sir William take Alexander away from school?
3. To whom does Alexander write letters?
4. Why is Mrs Milcote grateful to Mrs Lynch?
5. Who saves Melissa's baby, and how?

EXAM PRACTICE
Write a paragraph explaining how Alexander's voice breaking sets off a train of consequences.

**You must be able to:** write about how the friendship between Aaron and Toby develops.

## How do Chapters 15 and 16 introduce Aaron and Toby?

At the start of Part 2, Aaron and Toby are now eight and living fairly happily in the Coram Hospital. In an episode revealing their friendship, they sneak out one night to test the rumour that an old woman known as Mother Catbrain is a witch who can turn into a cat. They throw stones at her and conclude that she has done so.

Later Aaron retrieves Mother Catbrain's bucket for her and she reads his palm, telling him he is a gentleman (not a commoner).

We learn that Aaron's foster mother loved him like her own child, despite which he had to return to Coram. Toby wants to go to America to find his mother. He hates being treated as a plaything at parties because he is black.

Aaron goes to the chapel to hear music, and meets the composer Handel, who discovers Aaron's musical talent. Alexander arrives, unaware that Aaron is his son.

## How does Chapter 17 reunite Thomas and Alexander?

When Thomas Ledbury visits musician Mr Burney to discuss Handel's wish that Aaron should be apprenticed to him, he is delighted to meet his old friend Alexander, now a musician and living in Burney's house.

## How are Aaron and Toby separated in Chapters 18 and 19?

The two friends receive contrasting news: Toby is going to be a servant in the household of Philip Gaddarn (really Otis Gardiner), who treats his servants badly, and whom Toby says is not 'a moral man'; Aaron is to be apprenticed to the musician Mr Burney. The boys talk about running away together, and confide in the blind Mercy, but their plans are unrealistic. Moreover, Aaron realises that he wants to be a musician 'more than anything else in the world' – which reveals his similarity to his father, Alexander. Mercy advises against running away. Toby doubts Aaron's friendship, but Aaron insists: 'I am always your friend.'

In Chapter 19 the two boys are summoned to see Coram's kindly housekeeper Mrs Hendry, and think they are in trouble because of a fight with another boy, but Mrs Hendry wants to tell them that they are moving on from Coram. She takes out a tray of tokens left by mothers with their babies and gives Toby the beads his mother left him and the fine christening robe and silver locket left with Aaron (by Mrs Milcote). Both boys are moved by these tokens.

The boys are told they will still be able to come back and visit Mish (Meshak).

## Key Quotations to Learn

'A gentleman you were born, a gentleman you are and a gentleman you will be.'
(Mother Catbrain to Aaron: Chapter 15)

… he remembered how he had clung to her skirts screaming (Aaron recalls
Mrs Camberwell: Chapter 16)

Toby liked Mr Ledbury. Everyone did. (Chapter 18)

## Summary

- Aaron and Toby throw stones at Mother Catbrain. On another occasion she tells
  Aaron he is a gentleman.
- Aaron's foster mother loved him, but he was torn from her to go back to Coram.
- Toby hates being treated as a plaything by wealthy women he serves at parties.
- The composer Handel discovers Aaron's musical talent. Alexander is working with
  him, which leads to him being reunited with Thomas.
- Aaron and Toby are told they will leave Coram – Toby to be Philip Gaddarn's
  servant, and Alexander to be apprenticed to a musician.
- Prior to their departure, Mrs Hendry gives the boys tokens of their mothers.

## Questions

QUICK TEST
1. What is popularly believed about Mother Catbrain?
2. Through which third person are Alexander and Thomas reunited?
3. How does the composer Handel feature in Aaron's life?
4. Where do Aaron and Toby fantasise about going together?
5. What does Mrs Hendry give Aaron and Toby?

EXAM PRACTICE
Write a paragraph about how friendship features in the plot of these chapters.

# Chapters 20 to 24

**You must be able to:** analyse how the plot leads towards Gaddarn being exposed as Otis.

## How do Aaron and Toby's lives change in Chapters 20–24?

Toby is distressed as he is taken away to Gaddarn's house. Aaron weeps to lose his friend, but Mercy soothes him. He says goodbye to Mish, and is led to London by Mr Burney's housekeeper. He meets his roommate Timothy.

Mr Burney puts Aaron through musical tests and is pleased with him. By quite a coincidence – or fate – Alexander will become Aaron's teacher. At first he is thrown by Aaron singing 'The Silver Swan' – the song that Alexander once sang at Ashbrook.

Chapter 21 begins with Meshak 'being dead' because he is once again visited by visions of dead babies. However, Aaron returns and tells him he will visit Coram once a week to practise singing Handel's *Messiah*. Aaron also manages to see Toby sometimes while Timothy is watching the singer Nancy Dawson. Sometimes Mrs Bellamy helps him to spend time with Aaron. On one such occasion they see African slaves. This prompts Aaron to ask Toby if Gaddarn still beats him. Toby says he beats 'all of us', and that he hates Gaddarn.

At Gaddarn's party, Alexander, as its musical director, sees a reluctant Toby being petted by ladies. When Gaddarn talks about selling Toby into slavery, Alexander looks at him with disgust, and knows he has seen him before.

## How does Toby find out about Gaddarn's criminal business?

At Gaddarn's party, Toby is exhausted and falls asleep in a side room, but is woken by the voices of Gaddarn and some business associates. They discuss how Gaddarn will procure Coram children to become slaves or join harems. He also reveals a secret trapdoor opening onto a chamber and a tunnel leading to the Thames.

After Gaddarn and his cronies have gone, Toby opens the trapdoor, and asks himself, 'How can I save the Coram children? Who will believe me?'

## How does the plot lead towards Gaddarn's crimes being exposed?

Aaron enjoys learning about music, and Alexander is to have an opera performed. One day, however, Aaron dreams of Toby and knows he must visit him. Toby tells him about Gaddarn's business, and shows him where the tunnel emerges. Toby has just recovered from an illness. Mrs Bellamy has been dismissed for 'neglecting her duties' to look after him.

Alexander and Burney attend the first performance of Handel's *Messiah*, as does Gaddarn. Alexander realises at last that Gaddarn is in fact Otis Gardiner. Meshak attracts attention by loudly applauding Aaron.

Afterwards, Alexander tells Thomas about his discovery. Thomas says Gaddarn cannot be Otis, because he was hanged for 'murder, extortion, fraud and blackmail', and that Admiral

Bailey was charged with conspiracy. The scandal emerged because Theodore Claymore's ward spoke out when Otis tried to blackmail her.

It becomes apparent that Gaddarn is Otis Gardiner, and Mish is his son Meshak.

## Key Quotations to Learn

'I think young Master Dangerfield and I will get on like a house on fire.' (Alexander talking about Aaron: Chapter 20)

It all came back with such terrifying intensity that the only way he could escape the visions and sounds was to be dead. (Meshak: Chapter 21)

… he couldn't imagine feeling any happier on this earth, unless it was to discover his mother and father. (Aaron: Chapter 23)

## Summary

- Toby is taken to Gaddarn's house; Aaron goes to be apprenticed to Burney. He becomes pupil to Alexander (his own father!).
- Aaron will visit Meshak. He is also able to spend some time with Toby, who hates Gaddarn.
- At Gaddarn's party, Alexander realises he has seen Gaddarn before.
- Toby overhears Gaddarn discussing the sale of Coram children.
- Toby tells Aaron about Gaddarn's criminal activities. At Handel's *Messiah*, Alexander becomes convinced that Gaddarn is Otis, even though Thomas says Otis was hanged.

## Questions

QUICK TEST
1. What song does Aaron sing to Mr Burney?
2. How does Alexander come to see and recognise Gaddarn?
3. How does Toby find out about Gaddarn's criminal trade?
4. At what event does Meshak hear Aaron sing?
5. Why does Thomas say that Gaddarn cannot be Otis?

EXAM PRACTICE
Write a paragraph about how these chapters lead towards Gaddarn's crimes being exposed.

**You must be able to:** analyse how the Coram boys' visit to Ashbrook creates both hope and danger.

## How does Melissa come to see her son?

Melissa feels 'trapped in the past' because of her secret grief and her mother's refusal to discuss it. She no longer trusts Mrs Lynch, whom she suspects of sharing a secret with her mother. Mrs Milcote now runs the Ashbrook orphanage, and Melissa works there. She lives in Waterside to prevent bringing infections back to Ashbrook.

Thomas brings news that Alexander is well, and gives Melissa a letter from him saying that his feelings for her are unchanged. She replies in a friendly tone, but does not tell him about Aaron. Thomas arranges for a group of six Coram boys, including Aaron, to come to Ashbrook to perform music from Handel's *Messiah*, and to give a concert in the village. Melissa is delighted (though she does not know her own son will be coming), but Mrs Milcote is anxious.

## How does the Coram boys' visit to Ashbrook progress the plot?

The boys arrive, accompanied by Meshak, who is desperate to see 'his angel' Melissa. He is conflicted about telling her the truth. He feels that Aaron belongs to him, and is the only way he can have a part of Melissa. He goes into the wood and imagines dead babies, and feels 'shunned' by the angels because of his guilt.

At Ashbrook, Alexander's parents are moved when Aaron sings 'The Silver Swan'. Mrs Milcote is so upset she has to go to her room. In the night she goes to look at Aaron and is struck by his resemblance to Alexander, but she believes that Aaron has been murdered. She feels terrible guilt, but then confesses to Melissa.

## How does the suspense increase as a result of the Coram boys' concert?

Sir William admits to Thomas that he regrets his treatment of Alexander and wants a reconciliation. Thomas takes a letter from him to deliver to Alexander.

The Coram boys' benefit concert is a success, but Melissa is preoccupied, feeling betrayed by her mother, who is obsessed by her deep regret over Melissa's baby. As Thomas, Meshak and the Coram boys leave for London, Mrs Milcote recognises Meshak and runs desperately after the coach, calling out his name and crying, 'What happened to the child?', before collapsing and dying. When Aaron asks about 'that woman', Meshak lies to him. Fearing capture and the loss of Aaron, Meshak speaks harshly to him for the first time: 'Enough of that, you brat!' Aaron recoils 'as if he had been burnt'.

When Ashbrook's estate manager, sent by Sir William, catches up with the coach, Meshak fears detection and runs away with an anxious Aaron, stealing milk on the way to sustain them both. He is relieved to arrive at the Thames, knowing it will lead them to London.

## Key Quotations to Learn

'We are both grieving, but you won't allow me to help you, and you won't help me.' (Melissa to her mother: Chapter 25)

He only thought how Aaron belonged to him. Melissa could never be his but he could always have her son. (Meshak: Chapter 25)

'I did not truly know till now how much I loved my son and miss him.' (Sir William: Chapter 27)

## Summary

- Melissa cannot resolve her grief because her mother refuses to discuss their loss. Thomas brings her a letter from Alexander, but she does not tell Alexander about their baby.
- Thomas arranges for six Coram boys, including Aaron, to give a concert in Ashbrook.
- Sir William regrets his treatment of Alexander and wants him to return.
- Mrs Milcote confesses to Melissa, who feels betrayed. Mrs Milcote recognises and pursues Meshak, but drops down dead.
- Sir William sends a man after Meshak, who escapes with Aaron.

## Questions

QUICK TEST
1. Who feels 'trapped in the past'?
2. Why does Meshak feel 'shunned' by the angels?
3. How has Sir William's attitude changed?
4. What is Mrs Milcote doing when she dies?
5. Why does Meshak run away with Aaron a second time?

EXAM PRACTICE
Write a paragraph explaining what key character developments take place in these chapters.

# Chapters 29 to 32 and Epilogue

**You must be able to:** analyse how the novel reaches its final **climax**.

## How do Alexander and Melissa begin to suspect that Aaron is their son?

The Ashbrook family and Melissa attend Mrs Milcote's funeral. Melissa sees a portrait of Alexander as a boy and mistakes it for Aaron. She points out the similarity to Isobel, watched by a snake-eyed Mrs Lynch.

Alexander returns for the funeral and is reunited with the grieving Melissa. The next day they and Isobel share their information, leading Alexander to ask Melissa: 'Is the Coram boy, Aaron Dangerfield, our son?'

## How does the net tighten around Gaddarn/Otis?

Gaddarn hosts a party but is not in a party mood. He has seen Meshak at Handel's *Messiah* and now dreads being identified as Otis Gardiner. He tries to reassure himself, but finds out that Meshak has fled Ashbrook with one of the Coram boys, and worries more, taking his mood out on Toby.

Toby escapes the attentions of the ladies and hides. Meanwhile, Meshak (Mish) appears, with Aaron, asking for his father, naively expecting his help. Toby sees them locked in the map room, escapes through a cellar, and runs to Mr Burney's house to tell him and Thomas that Gaddarn has Aaron and Mish, and will 'send 'em to be slaves just like all the others'.

## What leads up to Alexander and Thomas confronting Gaddarn?

Chapter 31 backtracks to how Meshak and Aaron reached London and arrived at Gaddarn's house, with Meshak hoping for help, only for them to be locked up. Even after Gaddarn insists he is not Meshak's father, and viciously kicks him in the head, Meshak still hopes that Gaddarn will help him to keep Aaron.

Far from helping, Gaddarn smuggles Meshak and Aaron to the docks and puts them on a slave ship bound for America. This, arguably, is the novel's **crisis** point. When Toby rushes down the quayside, leading Alexander and Thomas to the ship, he is also captured, and Alexander and Thomas are surrounded by sailors. Fearing that he will lose Aaron, Meshak knocks Alexander unconscious. When Gaddarn lunges at his prostrate body with his sword, Thomas takes 'the brunt of the murderous thrust'. This is the novel's climax.

The ship sails with Meshak, Aaron and Toby, and Alexander is left 'lying on the quay with Thomas sprawled like a shield across his chest'.

Aaron and Toby seem doomed, but a sailor knocks Toby overboard and Aaron jumps after him. However, Chapter 31 ends with fishermen preparing to save them.

# How does the novel wind down to a conclusion?

Alexander and Melissa visit Mrs Milcote's grave, and Alexander visits that of Thomas. Aaron arrives at Ashbrook with Toby and tells Alexander he thinks he is his son. In the **Epilogue**, an ageing Meshak reflects on his life, and prepares to meet his mother in the afterlife.

## Key Quotations to Learn

'Who am I? A mother without a child, a child without a mother.' (Melissa: Chapter 29)

Mr Gaddarn moved among his guests, his eyes hooded and watchful, like a swordsman having to watch his front and back. (Chapter 30)

The pain of the knowledge, the excitement of knowing, tore at his guts, pitching his emotions like the waves of the sea. (Aaron: Chapter 31)

## Summary

- Alexander arrives for Mrs Milcote's funeral. He and Melissa think Aaron may be their son.
- Gaddarn fears exposure, especially when Meshak turns up with Aaron.
- Toby escapes and fetches Mr Burney and Thomas to save Aaron and Meshak.
- Gaddarn locks Meshak and Aaron up, then smuggles them onto a slave ship.
- Meshak knocks Alexander out. Gaddarn tries to stab him; Thomas dies protecting him.
- The ship sets sail, but Toby is pushed overboard, followed by Aaron. Fishermen prepare to rescue them. Aaron and Toby reach Ashbrook.
- The novel ends with an elderly Meshak preparing to die peacefully.

## Questions

QUICK TEST
1. What sparks Melissa's suspicion that Aaron may be her son?
2. How do Alexander and Thomas know where Aaron and Meshak are?
3. Who knocks Alexander unconscious?
4. Who stabs Thomas?
5. How does Toby escape the slave ship?

EXAM PRACTICE
Write two paragraphs comparing brave and villainous behaviour in these chapters.

# Narrative Structure

**You must be able to:** analyse the novel's two-part structure.

## What story elements are set up in Part 1?

Part 1 begins in 1741. The first three chapters establish Otis Gardiner as a threat to Ashbrook. This first part also develops the friendship between Alexander and Thomas, and shows the start of Meshak's obsession with Melissa.

This part builds to a high point of tension and release in two stages. First, Alexander's father forces him to leave the choir school. This leads him to leave Ashbrook – after making love to Melissa. The second stage is the consequence: Melissa becomes pregnant, and her baby is given to Otis, then saved by Meshak.

## How does Part 2 develop to a climax and resolution?

This part begins in 1750. Melissa's baby, Aaron, is now an eight-year-old at Coram, and is friends with Toby. Both are watched over by Mish (Meshak). Alexander and Thomas have established themselves in musical careers.

Otis Gardiner, meanwhile, has managed to have someone else hanged in his place, and has reinvented himself as Gaddarn.

Trouble develops in Chapters 18–19 when Aaron and Toby are separated and Toby is sent to serve Gaddarn. This is pivotal, as it is Gaddarn saying that he will sell Toby into slavery that makes Alexander realise that he looks familiar. It is also Toby who overhears Gaddarn discussing his human trafficking, and who eventually runs for help when Gaddarn puts Aaron and Meshak on the slave ship.

The storylines of Otis/Gaddarn and Meshak, and those characters associated with Ashbrook, merge in the two-part climax of Chapter 32: Thomas dies defending Alexander; Aaron and Toby escape the slave ship.

The climax is followed by the **falling action** of Chapter 32, which reveals the characters' losses and gains.

## How does the novel create suspense and dramatic tension?

The novel creates and releases tension. For example, the tension created by Sir William's opposition to Alexander's music is released by Alexander leaving Ashbrook, but it is not yet resolved, because Alexander leaves Melissa pregnant, and he is lost to his family for nine years.

The novel also raises questions. Will Alexander return? Will he and Melissa be reunited? Will Aaron survive? Will he find his parents? Will Otis face justice?

Tension is relaxed at times before being wound up again. Thus, after the drama at the end of Part 1, we have the relatively calm Chapters 15–17, in which we see Aaron and Toby as friends, Aaron apprenticed and Alexander flourishing.

This process is enriched by foreshadowing through which the author hints at later events. For example, when Thomas glimpses Meshak spying in Chapter 8, he is 'filled with unease', which alerts the reader to danger.

## What is the purpose of the Epilogue?

The Epilogue provides closure. The novel begins with Meshak being bullied, and he is a pivotal character, so it is appropriate that the novel ends with him. In fact the author has said that her first version of the novel began with what is now the Epilogue, with the whole story being told as a **flashback**.

The Epilogue shows that Meshak has in part come to terms with his murders. It also tells us that his greatest happiness remains being able to see Melissa, Aaron and Toby.

## Key Quotations to Learn

Thomas shuddered. Filled with unease, he closed the shutters. (Chapter 8)

'Mr Ashbrook ... I think I'm your son.' (Aaron to Alexander: Chapter 32)

Otis Gardiner ... had never been caught to face justice. (Chapter 32)

## Summary

- The novel is in two parts, roughly nine years apart.
- Part 1 leaves questions unanswered and tensions unresolved.
- Part 2 shows how the characters have changed in the eight years since Part 1 ended.
- In Part 2 the characters' lives entwine more closely, leading to climax and resolution.
- The falling action reveals the characters' losses and gains.
- The Epilogue gives closure.

## Questions

QUICK TEST
1. Over how many years in total is the novel spread?
2. How does Sir William create acute narrative tension?
3. What makes the start of Part 2 fairly calm?
4. What two things does Meshak do that are pivotal to the plot?
5. Who does the Epilogue focus on?

EXAM PRACTICE
Draw a storyline and indicate on it what you consider to be the five or six key moments in the novel.

**You must be able to:** understand how Gavin creates and contrasts these settings.

## How is rural Gloucestershire depicted?

The novel begins with Otis and Meshak travelling through rural Gloucestershire – where the author has lived for many years. They are in a mule-drawn wagon – a standard mode of commercial transport in the middle of the eighteenth century – and trying to make the ferry at Framilode, to cross the River Severn in order to reach Gloucester; there was no Severn Bridge then.

The Cotswold Hills were known as a wild, even dangerous, area. Meshak is a fearful youth, but is justified in fearing 'the real world of robbers and highwaymen, especially near the forest'.

There was no motorised travel, so distances in the novel seem longer than they would nowadays. One Gloucester choirboy comes from 'as far away as Dursley'. This journey would only take 35 minutes by car, but would have taken six hours on foot. Even travel by wagon could be difficult, as we see in Chapter 4 when Otis's wagon gets stuck in the mud.

Gavin paints a picture of a wild but beautiful countryside of 'thick beechwoods, where knotted roots thrust up through the earth'. Often this comes in glimpses, as when Thomas falls from his horse.

## How are rural poverty and wealth contrasted?

Jamila Gavin witnessed poverty as a child in India. In England in 1750 there was no **welfare state**. Rural life may have been healthier than city life, but poverty could still be extreme, as represented by the Ashbrook orphanage before Lady Ashbrook reforms it. She and a friend are shocked by its 'filth and rubbish and … young children … who scratched continuously and listlessly'.

Similar poverty is represented by Mother Catbrain, who inhabits a windowless 'hovel' whose 'piercing gaps' are 'stuffed with rags'. This poverty is far removed from the world of Ashbrook, which from a distance looks like a 'hidden kingdom' dominated by 'the finest house Thomas could ever have imagined'.

## How is Gloucester presented?

Gloucester has a cathedral with a choir. Meshak loves to visit the cathedral's angels. As a city, Gloucester mingles the elegant and the seedy: 'the stench of open sewers and foraging pigs … intermingled with women's perfume and polished leather'. The Black Dog inn, 'choking with smoke and stuffiness', is an appropriate place for Otis. Sailors are 'entwined with young women' and the barmaids do not mind being pulled onto Otis's knee. In a back room Mrs Peebles deals in illegitimate babies.

## How are London and Coram represented?

London is sophisticated enough for the debut performance of Handel's *Messiah* to be sold out, but there is also more low-brow entertainment such as that offered by singer Nancy Dawson, beloved of Timothy. It houses cultured people like Mr Burney, but it is also the setting for crime and corruption, represented by Gaddarn. Its dangerous docklands are, appropriately, where he murders Thomas.

The Coram Hospital was in Bloomsbury, now in central London, but still surrounded by fields in the 1750s. When Martha takes Aaron to London, they walk for an hour before the 'sweet-smelling fields gave way to the stench, smoke and smells of city streets'. Coram is a healthy place to be brought up, yet close enough to London for Gaddarn to visit it to choose children to sell.

## Key Quotations to Learn

Beautiful ornamental gardens were bursting with summer flowers and elegant walks entered shady pergolas and secret bowers. (Ashbrook: Chapter 4)

... a filthy yard running with excrement and manure (Ashbrook orphanage: Chapter 6)

... a blur of wild orchids and buttercups and purple scabious (Seen by Thomas: Chapter 7)

## Summary

- Rural Gloucestershire is wild and beautiful, rather dangerous, and in places very poor. Gavin has lived in Gloucestershire for many years.
- Ashbrook's orphanage shows rural poverty at its worst. Gavin saw poverty in India.
- Ashbrook is contrasted with poverty elsewhere.
- The cities, especially London, are more sophisticated, but still have filth and corruption.
- The Coram Hospital was in countryside outside of London.

## Questions

QUICK TEST
1. Where are Otis and Meshak trying to reach in Chapter 1?
2. What does Meshak justifiably fear in the Cotswolds?
3. Which setting is 'like a hidden kingdom'?
4. What tragic incident occurs in London's docklands?
5. Where was the Coram Hospital?

EXAM PRACTICE
Write two paragraphs comparing two settings in the novel and what they represent – for example, the Black Dog inn and Ashbrook.

# Eighteenth-Century Society

**You must be able to:** understand how the context of the eighteenth century influences the novel.

## How are social class and inequality depicted in the novel?

The novel reflects the social inequality of the period. Sir William and Lady Ashbrook live in a magnificent house on an elegant estate in the Cotswolds, with servants and estate workers. Their wealth is inherited, but Sir William manages the estate to increase it, and expects Alexander to do the same. Thomas reflects in Chapter 8 on the irony of wealth restricting Alexander rather than giving him freedom to do what he wants.

Contrasted with this wealth is the desperate poverty of the Ashbrook orphanage and of Mother Catbrain. Even Thomas, son of a ship's carpenter, is poor compared with Alexander. His large family lives in a two-room cottage and his uncle's best clothes are a source of shame at Ashbrook.

The novel displays a distinction between the 'gentleman' class and ordinary people. The choirboys are aware that Alexander is a gentleman and treat him with a certain respect.

Another social development is shown by Otis/Gaddarn. In 1750 Britain was at the very start of the **Industrial Revolution**. Otis is lower-class – a wandering pedlar. Alexander calls him 'insolent', implying that he lacks respect for his 'betters'. However, he makes enough money through crime to own a 'fashionable' London house and throw lavish three-day parties. People assume he has made his money through trade or industry. This kind of **social mobility** was becoming possible at this time.

## How are eighteenth-century gender roles shown?

The novel reflects eighteenth-century women's lack of power. Lady Ashbrook has some power on the orphanage committee, but she is ruled by her husband on most matters.

Some women achieved financial independence through widowhood. This may be the case with Mrs Peebles at the Black Dog inn. Mrs Lynch is presumably a widow, and perhaps would nowadays be a successful businesswoman. She wields power and supplements her housekeeper's income by involvement in Otis's trade and by blackmailing Mrs Milcote.

A few women had jobs in caring or organisational roles, as do Mrs Lynch and Martha Baines, and Mrs Hendry at Coram. Mrs Milcote, Lady Ashbrook's poor relative, works as a governess to the Ashbrook children.

Another aspect of gender in the novel is that young unmarried women who become pregnant are the ones who face shame and social isolation, not the men involved.

## How are children treated?

Children in the eighteenth century had few rights. The neglect of poor children is seen in the Ashbrook orphanage, where many babies died within a few weeks.

Meshak is 14 at the start of the novel, but remains childlike all his life. He is beaten and neglected by Otis, but is treated more humanely at Coram. Aaron is fortunate that his musical talent is recognised, but when he is apprenticed, at the age of eight, he has to work hard, and knows that otherwise he could be on the streets. Other children in the novel are far less fortunate, like those sold by Otis to provide 'cheap – if not slave – labour' in mills and on farms, and Toby, overworked and beaten by Gaddarn.

## Key Quotations to Learn

'You are normal for your kind and I for mine.' (Thomas to Alexander: Chapter 4)

He, Thomas, who had nothing, was free to follow a life of music, while Alexander, who had everything, was imprisoned by his wealth and class. (Chapter 8)

Some said he was a new mill owner from the Midlands, others said no, he came from the North and owned ships. (Gaddarn: Chapter 21)

## Summary

- There were huge inequalities of wealth and opportunity.
- Social mobility was increasing, as shown by Gaddarn.
- Few jobs were open to women, other than those of housekeeper or governess.
- Widows who had inherited property were more independent.
- Children could be beaten or treated virtually as slaves.

## Questions

QUICK TEST
1. How did Sir William acquire his wealth?
2. What does Thomas find ironic about Alexander's background?
3. How does Otis/Gaddarn reflect 'social mobility'?
4. What jobs were available to women?
5. What happened within a few weeks to many babies taken to Ashbrook orphanage?

EXAM PRACTICE
Write one or two paragraphs about how Gavin uses the eighteenth-century setting to present the key theme of inequality.

# Race and Slavery

**You must be able to:** understand how racial issues and slavery enter into the novel.

## What was Britain's role in the slave trade?

By 1750 Britain was trading more slaves than any other nation. It took slaves from West Africa to the Caribbean and America, which was a British colony until 1783. Britain and Portugal together transported around three million slaves.

A **triangular trade** developed, in which ships carried goods such as guns, alcohol and textiles from Britain to West Africa. Their captains would then rove up and down the coast buying slaves supplied by African traders from further inland. When a ship was full it would sail for America or the Caribbean – the West Indies. Many slaves in America worked on cotton plantations, most in the Caribbean on sugar plantations. Ships would sail back to Britain with sugar, cotton and other goods.

The 1799 Slave Trade Act limited the trade to London, Liverpool and Bristol. These cities became rich from the slave trade, which was not abolished until 1807. At the time when *Coram Boy* is set, there were about 1,500 black people living in England, mostly in these three cities. Most worked as domestic servants. Some, like Toby, worked in wealthy homes, where they were regarded as an exotic novelty.

## How were slaves treated?

Slaves were transported in appalling conditions, chained in darkness in the holds of ships, as are those depicted by Gavin in Chapter 31. Many died on the way. Some threw themselves overboard if they got the chance, as Toby intends to do. Some pregnant women found a way to abort their child rather than bring it into a life of slavery.

Toby could be said to be fortunate compared with other children born to enslaved parents: by the end of the novel his prospects look much better than they would have done in slavery – even if he had survived. The reader can only guess what will happen to him after he arrives at Ashbrook. In the Epilogue, Meshak still sees him there along with Melissa and Aaron. He might have been brought up alongside Aaron. He has at least escaped the threat of Gaddarn selling him into slavery.

## Could slaves be freed in Britain?

Some of the British black population were freed slaves, like Old Benjamin, who tells Toby where Africa is. It is Benjamin's daughter who was paid by the Coram Hospital to be a wet nurse to the infant Toby. Though most black people worked as servants, some worked independently and even started businesses. Slavery was not officially recognised under British law, but many black people worked unpaid in conditions amounting to slavery.

## Key Quotations to Learn

… a group of black men and women, all chained together, shuffled by, shivering and all but naked. (Chapter 11)

There was nothing a wealthy family in society liked more than to have a little black boy as a plaything. He was such a pet, just like their lapdogs, only more enchanting. (Otis: Chapter 11)

They heard the slash of the whips, the clank of chains but, worst of all, the long, low, endless moaning … a moan from three hundred slaves, lying crammed, side by side, some barely living, some dreaming, some dying. (Chapter 31)

## Summary

- Britain was the nation that traded the most slaves.
- In 1799 slave trading was limited to London, Liverpool and Bristol, which all became rich.
- Ships took goods from Britain to West Africa, where they picked up slaves and took them to the West Indies and America. They then brought goods such as sugar and cotton back to Britain.
- There were about 1,500 black people in Britain in 1750.
- Slaves were transported in appalling conditions. Some were freed in Britain.

## Questions

QUICK TEST
1. What kind of plantations did slaves typically work on in the West Indies?
2. What did ships bring back from America for British mills?
3. How does Toby intend to escape slavery?
4. How does Otis know he will make money from Toby?
5. Which three cities were given a monopoly of the slave trade in 1799?

EXAM PRACTICE
Write a paragraph about how Toby is impacted by slavery and attitudes to race.

# Philanthropy and Charitable Institutions

**You must be able to:** explain how the novel reflects eighteenth-century philanthropy.

## What is philanthropy?

Philanthropy refers to charitable funding inspired by a love of humanity. The term is particularly applied to wealthy individuals – philanthropists – donating to what they consider worthy causes.

During the eighteenth century, some individuals who had become wealthy through trade or industry were prompted by their Christian belief to fund charities. Sometimes, however, their motives were mixed. They may have felt guilty about how their money was made, or they may have wanted to be praised. Gaddarn in the novel is an extreme example of this. He is admired as a Coram **benefactor**, but in fact sells its children into slavery.

## What was the Coram Hospital?

Officially known as the London Foundling Hospital, Coram was set up in 1739 to care for children abandoned by their parents because of illegitimacy or poverty. Its founder, Thomas Coram, was a retired sea captain who cared about abandoned children and worked for 17 years to raise money from the wealthy to set up the institution that features in the novel.

Coram Hospital required mothers to leave their babies in person, and they could be turned away if the baby seemed too weak to survive, or likely to infect others. The exception was a period of 'General Reception' between 1756 and 1760, when, in return for state support, it admitted all babies. During this period, some men made money by taking babies to the Coram Hospital, as Otis promises to do. However, the Hospital never employed anyone to do this.

Many babies were left with a memento from their mother, which might identify them if the mother or family ever came for the child. Hence Toby is left with some African beads, and Aaron with a silver locket containing a lock of Melissa's hair.

Babies were fostered out for five years, then returned to the Hospital. Aaron is cared for by Mrs Camberwell, who is like a mother to him, then torn from her in a way that seems cruel nowadays. Later, like other Coram children, he is apprenticed. The Hospital checked that children apprenticed or with employers were treated well. In the novel, Toby is mistreated but knows no one would believe it of Gaddarn.

## What motivated the Coram Hospital?

Coram's benefactors wanted children to receive Christian instruction, and contributed to the foundation out of Christian charity. However, philanthropy often had mixed motives. Benefactors wanted to improve children's lives, but also to turn them into useful, God-fearing members of society.

There was also a moral judgement behind the Hospital. Children were taught to read but not write, its governors feeling that '… they ought to submit to the lowest stations, and should not be educated in such a manner as may put them upon a level with the Children of Parents who have the Humanity and Virtue to preserve them, and the Industry to Support them.' So, even at Coram they were seen as inferior because they had been abandoned.

## Key Quotations to Learn

'These wretched people live Godless lives of idleness and vice. Like leeches, they bleed our communities.' (Admiral Bailey: Chapter 6)

… she ran down the track after him, shouting, 'Remember, I love you, little Aaron. I'll always love you, my dearest sweet boy, my baby!' (Mrs Camberwell: Chapter 16)

'… if you fail to take up the opportunities which are offered you, only God could preserve you from the crime, poverty and degradation which awaits any weak sinner.' (Mrs Hendry: Chapter 19)

## Summary

- Philanthropy is charitable funding by the wealthy.
- Thomas Coram campaigned for 17 years to fund the Foundling Hospital.
- During a period of four years some men made money by taking babies to the Foundling Hospital.
- Many people made a moral judgement on the poor or illegitimate.

## Questions

QUICK TEST
1. What is philanthropy?
2. What was the commonest motive behind eighteenth-century philanthropy?
3. What temporary Coram policy change made it possible to make money by promising to take babies there?
4. Which Ashbrook orphanage committee member says the poor have only themselves to blame?
5. What do many mothers leave with their babies at Coram?

EXAM PRACTICE
List four facts about the Coram Hospital used in the novel. Using one or two, write a paragraph about how Gavin has used them to present themes.

# The Gothic Genre

**You must be able to:** understand in what ways *Coram Boy* can be seen as a Gothic novel.

## What is a Gothic novel?

Horace Walpole wrote the first English novel in the Gothic **genre**, *The Castle of Otranto* (1764). The characteristics of Gothic novels are: mystery and fear; elements of the **supernatural**, such as ghosts – real or imagined; nightmares; romance; emotional distress; bondage – as in prisoners or slaves; and menacing villains.

## How does the supernatural appear in the novel?

In many ways *Coram Boy* is very realistic. However, Meshak lives half in the everyday world and half in a world of ghosts and angels. He could be seen as a **mystic** or as mentally ill. He is bullied and beaten – kept in bondage – and one interpretation is that this makes him escape into an imagined spirit world. He also 'sees' the ghosts of babies he has been forced to kill. This is seen most clearly in the Epilogue, when he begs for their forgiveness.

The psychological component in Meshak's visions becomes clear in several ways: he is quick to think that Melissa is 'his' angel; he becomes 'dead' when distressed; he has nightmares and has to keep himself from crying out for fear of a beating; these return, along with the ghosts of children, when Aaron is apprenticed.

Meshak is also linked to the supernatural when Melissa goes to drown herself in a pond, itself a very Gothic setting. She sees what turns out to be Meshak's reflection and thinks, 'It must be the devil himself, waiting' (Chapter 13).

## How is Mother Catbrain a Gothic figure?

The rumours about Mother Catbrain that both excite and terrify Aaron and Toby are the kind that have throughout history been attached to elderly women living alone. They have heard that she can turn herself into a cat, and when they injure her cat with a stone, and later see the old woman limping, they take this as proof.

Aaron shows bravery and kindness when he rescues her bucket. This is when, in true Gothic fashion, she reads his palm and mysteriously tells him that he is a gentleman – which proves true.

## How does Meshak become more of a Gothic figure?

Meshak is an outsider. Even though he is treated kindly at Coram, he has no friends his own age. But he is even more of an outsider when he spies on the children in the 'play cottage', Waterside, or when Thomas sees him lurking outside the house. A big, clumsy figure who lopes like an animal, he can only engage in the happiness of others by spying on them. He resembles a character from another Gothic novel – the 'creature' (or monster) in Mary Shelley's *Frankenstein*.

# Who is the Gothic villain?

Otis Gardiner, who becomes Philip Gaddarn, is an obvious Gothic villain. He is handsome and charming, and when he becomes Gaddarn there is a mystery about his identity: no one knows where he comes from or how he acquired his fortune. He is also unscrupulous in his readiness to kill babies and blackmail their mothers, and to sell Coram children into slavery. His use of a secret tunnel to the docks is also very Gothic.

## Key Quotations to Learn

... a place full of terrors; full of stories of ghosts and goblins and tales of suicide. (The pond in the woods: Chapter 13)

But she had mistaken him for a ghost or a demon or some unquiet spirit. (Melissa sees Meshak's reflection: Chapter 14)

On certain nights, when the moon was full, it was said she would turn herself into a black cat and consort with demons and witches. (Mother Catbrain: Chapter 15)

## Summary

- Gothic novels feature mystery, fear, the supernatural, horror and villainy.
- Meshak is a Gothic figure in that he has visions and is a feared outsider.
- Mother Catbrain is seen as a witch, and reads Aaron's palm.
- There are several Gothic settings and descriptions in the novel.
- Otis/Gaddarn is a Gothic villain.

## Questions

QUICK TEST
1. What are the main features of a Gothic novel?
2. How is Meshak like the creature (monster) in *Frankenstein*?
3. Whose ghosts does Meshak see?
4. What stops Melissa from taking her own life?
5. How is Gaddarn mysterious?

EXAM PRACTICE
Write a paragraph about how the supernatural is significant in the novel.

Meshak (Mish)

**You must be able to:** understand how Gavin presents the character of Meshak.

## Who is Meshak?

Meshak is the vulnerable and childlike son of Otis Gardiner. He puts up uncomplainingly with being neglected, mistreated and belittled by his father, who sees him as a burden. His mother is dead, so the only affection he receives is from his dog, Jester. Tall and gangly, with an overly large head of red hair, he is often 'jeered and sneered' at, and 'cuffed'.

His father whips him to wake him or speed him up. He also has fits when he is 'dead' for hours, not even responding to beating.

## What are Meshak's loves, hates and fears?

Meshak likes churches, and is moved by their music, though he cannot sing himself. He visits Gloucester Cathedral because he loves to see its stained-glass saints and angels – especially one angel whom he regards as his own. In his mind, she takes him to see his dead mother, which is a joy to him even though he cannot join her. When he has fits, he enters 'a paradise' (Chapter 3) where he meets his angel.

Forced to help his father by stopping the unwanted children from escaping, Meshak tries to shut out their misery in order to protect himself. He particularly hates having to bury babies in ditches.

He is afraid of robbers and wild animals, but also things that he imagines or 'sees' in the spirit world, such as 'trolls and witches' (Chapter 1) and, worse, the ghosts of dead babies. He also has terrible nightmares.

## What is Meshak's role in the novel?

In a **narrative** sense Meshak serves to show his father's cruelty and to highlight the horror of how he makes his living. However, Meshak begins to serve a more active role in Chapter 7 when he looks through a window of Ashbrook's play cottage and sees Melissa. He lets out a 'gasp of astonishment' because he thinks she is 'his' angel. Hence, when at the end of Chapter 9 he sees her kissing Alexander, he howls in anguish. When she has a baby nine months later, Meshak runs away with it instead of burying it in a ditch, and takes it to the safety of the Coram Hospital. This baby is Aaron. When Aaron is eight, Meshak kidnaps him, putting him in great danger by taking him to Gaddarn (Otis).

As a Gothic character, Meshak adds elements of mystery, unpredictability and the supernatural to the novel. However, he also shows that even someone who has buried live babies can find redemption and die in peace.

## Key Quotations to Learn

He shut his eyes so as not to witness their despair. (Chapter 2)

Meshak stepped out of his body and into a paradise where he would meet his Gloucester angel. (Chapter 3)

Deep inside his brain, Meshak stood in a wasteland beneath a black sky. It was a place of nothingness; of non-existence. (Chapter 10)

## Summary

- Meshak is at first an awkward, frightened, mistreated 14-year-old.
- He 'sees' ghosts of dead babies, but in his fits he joins 'his' angel in paradise.
- He becomes obsessed with Melissa, thinking she is his angel, then saves her baby, (Aaron), taking him to Coram. Meshak is allowed to stay there, and is known as 'Mish'.
- He kidnaps the eight-year-old Aaron and takes him back to London.
- Gaddarn (Otis Gardiner) throws him onto a ship bound for America.
- After a life in America, he returns, and can finally join his mother in paradise.

## Sample Analysis

Meshak's role is **ambiguous**. He deserves pity, but he is also a Gothic figure, like the *Frankenstein* 'monster' or 'creature', spying on the young people, frightening them, howling like an animal, and later running off with the baby. He becomes more of a threat when, eight years later, he kidnaps Aaron and takes him to London, thinking that his father will help: 'I have a da. And your da is meant to protect you, isn't he, angel?' The simple assumption shows his naivety.

## Questions

QUICK TEST
1. What does Meshak look like?
2. What does he feel about the babies?
3. Why does he take Aaron to Gaddarn?
4. How is Meshak like a character in Gothic fiction?
5. Where does Meshak spend most of his adult life?

EXAM PRACTICE
Write a paragraph analysing how Meshak is important in the novel.

**You must be able to:** understand how Gavin presents Otis/Gaddarn as a villain.

## How does Otis behave in Part 1?

First impressions are important, and Chapter 1 opens with a whole paragraph of Otis abusing and bullying Meshak: 'Oi! Meshak! Wake up you lazy dolt … Not that one, you nincompoop … Why was I so cursed with a son like you?' Otis always treats Meshak like this.

Otis has no compassion for anyone, least of all the 'brats' he deals in. He is not just neglectful, but actively cruel, whipping Meshak just to wake him, and, as Alexander points out, treating his mules 'abominably' (Chapter 4), even though he depends on them.

## How does Otis become successful?

Otis is self-confident, which Alexander interprets as his being 'insolent' (Chapter 4). He is also an enterprising opportunist, going from pedlar to child trafficker and blackmailer. We see this opportunism later when he offers to trade some 'brats' for the baby Toby because he knows there is 'money in black infant boys' (Chapter 11).

He is also good-looking, charming with women, and a convincing deceiver. At the end of Chapter 1, at the ferry, he responds immediately to the question 'Are you the Coram man?', and takes a baby from a 'gentlewoman … with a great show of reverence and concern, as if he would protect it with his life', telling Meshak, 'Look caring … till we're on the other side.'

At the Black Dog, he boldly pulls a willing barmaid onto his lap and slaps her bottom. He also flirts with Mrs Lynch, knowing she may be useful to him, but refrains from offering the pock-marked Mrs Peebles 'false flattery' because he knows she would scorn it. Instead he treats her as a clever businesswoman, giving her his cynical view of the Coram Hospital's funding: 'Money coming from the wealthy to salve their consciences and purchase their respectability' (Chapter 2).

## What is Otis/Gaddarn's role?

Otis's opportunism and ability to deceive become more obvious in his reinvention of himself as Gaddarn – after arranging for someone else to be hanged in his place. He is the Gothic villain and **antagonist** of the novel, presenting the greatest threat to its good characters, especially Alexander. Much of the suspense of Part 2 centres on whether his criminal business will be discovered. This becomes more likely once Toby overhears him discussing it, and when Alexander recognises him.

The fact that Gaddarn is never apprehended makes the point that corruption and evil still exist in the world, even though Aaron and Toby are now safe.

## Key Quotations to Learn

'Why I don't ditch you is more than I can say. Thank your lucky stars that blood is thicker than water.' (Otis to Meshak: Chapter 1)

He was born a wheeler-dealer, already knowing how to make himself useful, dependable and indispensable. (Otis to Meshak: Chapter 2)

… the shadow of Otis Gardiner still lingered and encircled the world like a menacing whirlwind whose terror had never been harnessed and who had never been caught to face justice. (Chapter 32)

## Summary

- Otis neglects, beats and whips Meshak.
- He is cruel to children and animals, and unscrupulous in selling children.
- He is a blackmailer.
- He arranges for someone else to be hanged in his place.
- As Gaddarn, he becomes rich as a child trafficker and slaver.

## Sample Analysis

There is little to be said in Otis's favour. True, he does not abandon Meshak as a child. He claims that this is because 'blood is thicker than water' – Meshak is family, but it could be because he provides unpaid labour. It is surprising that Otis ensures Meshak is fed well at the Black Dog inn. He also stops trying to beat Meshak into consciousness when Mrs Peebles says he has fits. Even as Gaddarn he does decide at the last moment to ship Meshak to America rather than kill him.

## Questions

QUICK TEST
1. Who says Otis treats his mules 'abominably'?
2. How does Otis show his ability to deceive at the ferry?
3. How does Otis escape justice to reinvent himself as Gaddarn?
4. What does Otis think of Coram's benefactors?
5. What happens to Gaddarn at the end of the novel?

EXAM PRACTICE
Write a paragraph explaining the significance of Gaddarn's involvement in the Coram Hospital.

# Alexander Ashbrook

**You must be able to:** understand how Gavin presents Alexander as a hero, the novel's **protagonist**.

## What is Alexander like as a teenager?

Alexander is serious, introverted and devoted to music. Given the task of introducing Thomas to the choir school, he sympathetically tells him how to escape bullying. He calls Otis 'insolent', but warmly introduces the working-class Thomas as his 'dearest friend'. As Lady Ashbrook points out, Thomas makes him more 'human' (Chapter 9).

Alexander can be enthusiastic, as when he leads Thomas scrambling up a hill to view Ashbrook. He is concerned when Thomas falls off his horse. He is also affectionate towards his younger siblings.

When forced to leave the choir school, he has enough sense of duty to try to obey his father, but then decides to abandon the family for a musical career. This shows courage and determination.

## How is Alexander presented as an adult?

We first see the adult Alexander as a 23-year-old who has spent five years struggling 'in poverty' abroad. Nonetheless he has stuck to his passion, and has been rewarded with the respect of Mr Burney and the composer Handel. By the beginning of Part 2 he largely lives by composing, but still occasionally works as a musical director, which is how he encounters Gaddarn.

When Alexander meets Aaron, he feels emotional conflict because Aaron reminds him of himself at the same age, but is then kind and encouraging.

## How does Alexander's relationship with Melissa develop?

Alexander gets to know Melissa in the holidays. He comments in Chapter 7, 'Melissa seems quite amiable, don't you think?' The perceptive Thomas replies, 'She's very pretty, if that's what you mean.' Alexander's understatement hides his feelings. In Chapter 9 they kiss, and in Chapter 12 Melissa – boldly or naively – visits Alexander in bed, apparently to suggest that he could play the virginals in Waterside. This leads to them making love before he leaves Ashbrook.

## What role does Alexander play in the closing chapters?

Alexander's keen observation makes him think Gaddarn looks familiar. This is prompted by his sympathetic nature: overhearing Gaddarn talk about selling Toby into slavery makes him turn 'in disgust' and look 'directly into Mr Gaddarn's face' (Chapter 21). Later he realises Gaddarn is Otis.

When Gaddarn kidnaps Aaron, Alexander bravely confronts him, but has the presence of mind to offer to speak in his defence to lessen his sentence to 'transportation rather than the gallows' (Chapter 31) – being sent to the British colonies in America rather than being hanged.

Finally, in Chapter 32, we see a sadder and wiser Alexander grieving for his friend, and feeling guilty about Melissa and their lost son.

## Key Quotations to Learn

… a dazed, inverted look, as if he lived more inside himself than outside. (Chapter 4)

They lay in each other's arms all through the rest of the night, not knowing where affection ended and passion began. (Alexander and Melissa: Chapter 12)

'I think young Master Dangerfield and I will get on like a house on fire.' (Alexander talking about Aaron: Chapter 20)

## Summary

- Alexander is a serious youth with a passion for music.
- He befriends Thomas despite their class differences.
- He comes to love Melissa, and fathers her child.
- He abandons Ashbrook and his family for music.
- He confronts Gaddarn and is devastated by Thomas's death.

## Sample Analysis

Arguably, Alexander should have considered the possible consequences of his making love with Melissa, and he was cruel to leave Ashbrook immediately afterwards. On the other hand, he is scarcely more than a boy, and feels that a life at Ashbrook would 'destroy' him. In addition, he does write letters to Melissa, which are destroyed, and when he eventually learns about the pregnancy he feels 'Melissa's broken heart, and … would strike his head with horror, weeping uselessly,' showing his love, compassion and remorse.

## Questions

QUICK TEST
1. How does Alexander get to know Thomas?
2. What proves that Alexander is not a snob?
3. What comment betrays that he is drawn to Melissa?
4. How do we know that he never forgot Melissa?
5. How does he try to persuade Gaddarn to give up Aaron?

EXAM PRACTICE
Plan an essay arguing for or against the view that Alexander is entirely noble.

**You must be able to:** understand how Gavin presents Thomas.

## What is Thomas like as a teenager?

Thomas is a working-class boy from a large family, the son of a ship's carpenter. He is musical, so is able to join the Gloucester choir school, but he does not share Alexander's serious passion for music. Rather, he enjoys it in a light-hearted way that fits with his ability to entertain. Alexander recognises this, and when Thomas is almost in despair because of the other boys' taunting, he gets Thomas to stop it by making them laugh. He is a natural mimic, a gifted storyteller, and can sing and play popular songs he has heard and performed in pubs. He can even play the spoons!

He is apprehensive about spending the holidays at Alexander's home, knowing that Alexander is 'a gentleman', but he is unprepared for Ashbrook's grandeur, and is at first daunted by the servants smirking at his lack of knowledge at the dinner table. However, he persists, and through his good humour, his ability to entertain and his humility, he becomes popular without even trying.

Thomas is also sensitive and perceptive. He immediately sees how the stiff Mrs Milcote looks down on him and prevents Melissa 'from doing more than giving a slight bob' when they meet (Chapter 4). Typically this makes him blush with embarrassment rather than feel resentful.

Thomas is happy to entertain the other children at Ashbrook with his impressions, songs and – notably – the story of Dawdley Dan (Chapter 5). Even when Thomas falls from a horse, it is typical of him that he apologises and blames himself rather than the horse.

## How is Thomas presented as an adult?

Thomas as an adult is very similar to Thomas as a teenager. He is much liked by the children at Coram, where he is choirmaster. He is cheerful and encouraging, and seems to be an effective teacher as well as an entertaining one. He is also a good organiser. He arranges Aaron's apprenticeship, and organises the Coram choir's benefit concert at Ashbrook.

When Thomas and Alexander meet again after nine years, they renew their friendship at once, and he still has the same effect on Alexander. Aaron notices: 'when they were together, they became like boys again, with Mr Ledbury cracking his jokes, just as he did with the Coram children, and Mr Ashbrook trying not to smile, yet suddenly laughing uncontrollably.'

## How does Thomas die?

When Toby goes to Mr Burney's house to fetch help to save Aaron, he finds Thomas there: 'Thomas strode forward and put a kindly arm on the boy's shoulder' (Chapter 30). He dies courageously, defending Alexander from Gaddarn: 'As the sword came down, Thomas threw himself over his friend. Without even a cry, he took the brunt of the murderous thrust.' He is buried at Ashbrook, his epitaph stating, '… no friend was truer, no man was ever more missed' (Chapter 32).

## Key Quotations to Learn

'He is the most splendid fellow that ever walked the earth and the funniest!' (Alexander on Thomas: Chapter 4)

'Sorry, Alex, I'm no rider, you know.' (Chapter 7)

Toby liked Mr Ledbury. Everyone did. He was young and funny and often made them laugh when he taught them hymns. (Chapter 18)

## Summary

- Thomas is the son of a ship's carpenter, and one of a large family.
- He becomes popular with the choirboys and at Ashbrook by being good-humoured and entertaining.
- He is a cheerful and effective choirmaster at Coram.
- He sacrifices his life to save Alexander.

## Sample Analysis

Gavin presents Thomas as a foil to Alexander. Whereas Alexander is serious and often distant, Thomas is light-hearted, easy-going and approachable. Alexander has a passion for musical composition, while Thomas has natural ability as a versatile entertainer and teacher. In narrative terms, Thomas's unhesitatingly loyal self-sacrifice at the end of the novel enables the happiness that Alexander and Melissa will eventually achieve.

## Questions

QUICK TEST

1. What does Thomas's father do for a living?
2. How does Thomas stop the other choirboys from bullying him?
3. How does Thomas react when he falls off his horse?
4. What does Aaron especially like about Thomas?
5. How does Thomas die?

EXAM PRACTICE

Using one or more of the 'Key Quotations to Learn', explain what makes Thomas so likeable.

**Sir William and Lady Ashbrook**

**You must be able to:** understand the roles played by Sir William and Lady Ashbrook.

## How does Lady Ashbrook help the orphanage?

Lady Ashbrook represents the compassionate, benevolent side of the aristocracy. Pampered at Ashbrook, she had rarely come into contact with the poor. Chapter 6, however, backtracks to an incident that inspired her to help them. She was riding with a friend, Mrs Forsythe, when they discovered an abandoned child. They fed and bathed her, then handed her over to the orphanage.

A few months later, not only did they find that the girl had died, they were also shocked by conditions at the orphanage and by its slovenly parish nurse. Lady Ashbrook resolved to change this, replacing the nurse, raising money for improvements, and, with Mrs Forsythe, forming a committee to run the orphanage. She now sits on the committee and involves herself with the poor, despite Sir William objecting that it is beneath her, and that the poor are not her concern.

## What is Lady Ashbrook's relationship with Alexander?

Alexander is Lady Ashbrook's 'adored' eldest child, and she has defended him against her husband. She has a love of music and sang to him as a child. She is moved by his musical performances in a way that her husband is not, but she now agrees that when Alexander's voice breaks he should give up the choir and come home to learn how to manage the estate. She now regards his 'obsession' with his 'wretched music … ungentlemanly', and thinks he should obey his father.

## What is Sir William's relationship with Alexander?

Sir William has no musical appreciation and regards Alexander's music as an indulgence. He thinks that for Alexander to become a man he must follow the family tradition and run the estate. He is a 'stern and conscientious father' who does not try to understand or appreciate his son. When he hears Alexander sing, he sneeringly breaks into slow clapping.

Not content with taking Alexander away from the choir school, he removes all musical instruments from the house. When the outraged Alexander complains, 'Why, why have you done this to me?' Sir William beats him, insisting, 'This is the only way I know to get that music madness out of your system' (Chapter 12).

When Alexander leaves Ashbrook, Sir William furiously disinherits him. It takes years, and Thomas's intervention, to make him regret his actions and welcome Alexander home.

## Key Quotations to Learn

She thought … that Alexander would repay her devotion with compliance and return willingly to Ashbrook to take up his proper position in obedience to his father's wishes. (Lady Ashbrook: Chapter 6)

'We must make amends and try to save other children from that hell.' (Lady Ashbrook: Chapter 6)

'You are a man – at least, I hope to make one of you.' (Sir William to Alexander: Chapter 12)

## Summary

- Lady Ashbrook found an abandoned child, whom she had taken to the orphanage.
- Awful conditions at the orphanage made Lady Ashbrook feel responsible for the poor.
- Lady Ashbrook adores Alexander but comes to agree with Sir William that he should give up music and learn to manage the estate.
- Sir William tries to 'cure' Alexander by banning music from the house and beating him.
- When Alexander leaves, Sir William disinherits him.

## Sample Analysis

Lady Ashbrook and Sir William differ in their attitudes towards Alexander. To his mother, Alexander is 'her adored son' whom she has tried to protect from his 'stern and conscientious father'. She can at least partly understand Alexander, because of her own love of music. Sir William, however, can only ridicule Alexander, regarding music as a waste of time that 'won't bring in the harvest', this practical phrase indicating his main concerns in life – typical of an aristocratic landowner of the time.

## Questions

QUICK TEST
1. What incident alerts Lady Ashbrook to the plight of the poor?
2. What three things does Lady Ashbrook do to improve the orphanage?
3. How does Alexander respond to musical instruments being removed from Ashbrook?
4. How could it be said that Lady Ashbrook lets Alexander down?
5. What does Sir William do when Alexander leaves Ashbrook?

EXAM PRACTICE
Explain how Lady Ashbrook shows the more caring face of the aristocracy.

# Isobel Ashbrook and Melissa Milcote

**You must be able to:** understand Melissa and her relationship with Isobel.

## What is the relationship between the girls before Alexander returns?

Isobel introduces Melissa to Alexander as her 'dearest friend'. They have only known each other a few weeks, but Isobel is a warm, effusive girl, and, as she explains, she was 'so lonely' without Alexander.

Melissa is slightly older, but also rather shy – and perhaps less confident as she is the poor relative living at Ashbrook because her mother is its governess – so the two characters may balance each other out. Isobel says they 'have such fun together' (Chapter 7).

## How does the girls' relationship change?

In Chapter 10, after the boys have returned to school, Isobel feels 'stirrings of jealousy'. Up until now, 'Alexander had always been Isobel's closest friend.' Isobel is confused: 'something had changed and she wasn't sure what.' She wonders, 'Had Melissa taken her place as her brother's confidante?' She is too young to realise that Melissa and Alexander have become romantically involved.

When Isobel finally explains that she was worried that Melissa might have quarrelled with Alexander, Melissa comes close to saying she is in love with him, but then only says they are 'good, good friends'. She also explains that she has had 'the flowers' – meaning her first period. Isobel is alarmed, but Melissa reassures her.

After sharing confidences, Isobel and Melissa become close again, and there is a moment of foreshadowing when they 'mother' a baby doll at the cottage. However, after Alexander leaves Ashbrook, Isobel blames Melissa. It is only after Melissa tells Isobel she is pregnant that the friendship is repaired, with the girls naively discussing how they will care for the baby.

## What happens when Melissa becomes pregnant?

At first Melissa thinks she is ill. When the maid Tabitha refers to her having a baby, Melissa is so shocked that she uncharacteristically slaps the maid. When she accepts the truth, she goes to drown herself to escape the shame (typical of the time) of unmarried motherhood, and is only saved by thinking Meshak's reflection is the devil.

When Isobel demands an explanation of Melissa's 'illness', Melissa confesses, expecting Isobel to hate her. Instead, the two embrace in love and forgiveness. They then enter a 'private, secret world which no one else could penetrate', fantasising about bringing up the baby.

What happens is far more brutal. Mrs Lynch gives the baby to Otis, and Mrs Milcote tells Melissa that it is dead, thinking that this will save Melissa from stigma and allow her to make a fresh start.

## Key Quotations to Learn

'Melissa is my dearest friend – my sister,' enthused Isobel. (Chapter 4)

'Is that why you didn't come out to say goodbye? Is it why you are so distant with me?' (Isobel to Melissa: Chapter 10)

'You could have stopped him. You've ruined our lives.' (Isobel to Melissa: Chapter 13)

## Summary

- Isobel and Melissa become close friends in a short time.
- Isobel worries that Melissa has replaced her as Alexander's closest friend.
- Melissa says she 'admires' Alexander. She also says she has had her first period.
- Melissa thinks she is ill, then learns that she is pregnant. She considers suicide, then confesses to Isobel. They fantasise about bringing up the baby.
- Melissa gives birth and the baby is given to Otis. She is told it died.

## Sample Analysis

Isobel and Melissa have a close relationship intensified by there being no other teenage girls at Ashbrook. Isobel's warmth overcomes Melissa's shyness. The friendship wavers briefly because of Melissa falling in love with Alexander, complicated by her having her first period – which at that time would have been a difficult thing for her to share. Isobel's impulsive nature is seen when Melissa shows her Alexander's letter and Isobel says she could have prevented him from leaving and has 'ruined' their lives, this word choice being typical of Isobel's passionate, uncompromising nature.

## Questions

QUICK TEST
1. How have Isobel and Melissa become friends?
2. How do the two girls' personalities differ?
3. Why does Isobel feel jealous?
4. What does Isobel angrily say Melissa could have prevented?

EXAM PRACTICE
Make a plan for an essay arguing that Isobel and Melissa are just as important in the novel as Alexander and Thomas.

**You must be able to:** comment on the friendship between Aaron and Toby.

## What is the relationship between the boys at first?

It is characteristic of Aaron and Toby's relationship that we first see them sharing an adventure, daring each other to approach Mother Catbrain. Aaron is 'the younger [but] the bolder' (Chapter 15). He is prepared to face the old woman alone; Toby has a different attitude: 'We go together or stay together.' Aaron shows similar independence when he returns Mother Catbrain's bucket.

The boys are inseparable, and plan to sail to America together. It is Aaron to whom Toby confides how much he hates Gaddarn and being treated like an exotic pet. He dreads being sent to Gaddarn permanently.

## How does the boys' relationship change?

When the time comes for the boys to leave Coram, Toby wants them to 'go far away and be together always' because they are 'best friends … brothers', but Aaron's attitude has shifted: 'the thought of fleeing across the ocean to Africa or America no longer seemed as appealing as before' (Chapter 18). This conflict between friendship and a passion for music echoes that of Alexander.

Faced with this change of heart, the weeping Toby declares that he will flee on his own.

## How do the boys' lives diverge, then come together again?

For a while the boys' fortunes go in opposite directions. While Toby is miserable with Gaddarn – who talks of selling him into slavery – Aaron is happily progressing as Mr Burney's apprentice. He is also getting to know his father, although neither of them realises it.

Although Aaron has so far seemed the bolder of the two, Toby shows courage and initiative when, exhausted at one of Gaddarn's parties, he hides in the map room and overhears Gaddarn discussing child trafficking. He fights an impulse to do nothing, and makes himself look into Gaddarn's secret tunnel. He also shows a sense of responsibility: 'What should I do? Who shall I tell? How can I save the Coram children?' (Chapter 22).

When Aaron is at risk of being sold into slavery by Gaddarn, he is saved by Toby's loyalty and determination. Toby escapes the house and runs for help. Unfortunately, his impulsive nature makes him run 'rashly' onto the ship to join Aaron. Finally, it is Toby who sees how to get on deck, and who is about to jump overboard rather than be enslaved. When he is knocked overboard, Aaron's loyalty is instant: 'he just tipped himself over the side.'

## Key Quotations to Learn

'We could go on the ships to America or Africa, couldn't we, Aaron? And I could find my mother.' (Toby: Chapter 18)

'Don't run away, Toby. All you have to do to be free is grow up.' (Mercy: Chapter 18)

… he wanted to be a musician more than anything else in the world. (Aaron: Chapter 18)

## Summary

- Aaron and Toby are firm friends. Aaron is younger, but more independent. He has doubts about running away with Toby once he realises he wants to be a musician.
- Aaron does well with Mr Burney; Toby hates working for Gaddarn.
- Toby discovers Gaddarn's criminal trade and knows it is up to him to stop it.
- Meshak takes Aaron to Gaddarn and they are thrown onto a ship.
- Toby fetches help, but the ship sails with both boys. A sailor knocks Toby overboard; Aaron jumps after him.

## Sample Analysis

Although only eight, Gavin shows that Aaron experiences the same kind of passion for music that his father felt. It comes to him 'like a blinding flash', showing its suddenness and force. He also feels a similar emotional conflict. He wants to follow his passion, but 'not to be separated from Toby', so he feels 'confusion'. Toby has no such conflict: he loves his friend and hates Gaddarn.

## Questions

QUICK TEST
1. Who says, 'Well you go back, if that's what you want. I'm staying.'
2. Why does Toby want to go to America?
3. Why does Aaron have doubts about running away with Toby?
4. What does Toby overhear that makes him concerned about the Coram children?
5. Why is Toby about to jump overboard?

EXAM PRACTICE
Write a paragraph about how Gavin presents Aaron's similarity to Alexander.

**You must be able to:** comment on the roles played by other characters.

## What part does Mrs Milcote play?

Margaret Milcote is Melissa's mother. She is a widowed relative of Lady Ashbrook who has had to accept the job of Ashbrook's governess. Perhaps her inferior status has made her all the more concerned about class differences and acceptable upper-class behaviour, because she is described as 'stiff', barely acknowledges working-class Thomas, and tries to make Melissa and Isobel behave in an 'appropriate' way for aristocratic young ladies.

We see her coldness when she discovers the children being entertained by Thomas, and reprimands 'Miss Ashbrook', 'her words freezing like icicles as they left her pursed lips'.

Mrs Milcote's stiff and chilly personality makes it impossible for her to explain periods to Melissa. This, coupled with her terror of social disgrace, makes her pretend that Melissa's baby has died, and then refuse to speak about it. She only shows a more human side – regret – years later when she runs after Meshak and then drops dead.

## What roles do Mrs Peebles and Mrs Lynch play?

Mrs Peebles owns the Black Dog inn. She is a mysterious woman, keeping herself veiled and poorly lit to hide her smallpox scars, and involved in illegal deals with Otis. She is rumoured to have been a spy, and is alert to any opportunity for profit.

Mrs Lynch, the housekeeper at Ashbrook, is quite similar to Mrs Peebles in character. Like Mrs Peebles she has a nose for profit, as we see when she eavesdrops on Mrs Milcote and Melissa and concludes that Mrs Milcote wants her daughter to marry Alexander. When she realises that Melissa is pregnant, she begins to scheme, working out how to use this to her own advantage. She is a cold and unscrupulous woman: even after Mrs Milcote dies, it seems she intends to carry on blackmailing Melissa instead. True to character, when she fears being found out, she disappears 'mysteriously' (Chapter 30).

## What more benign female characters are there?

In contrast to Mrs Peebles and Mrs Lynch, Mrs Hendry, Coram's housekeeper, is firm but kind-hearted, being described as 'like a mother hen' as she checks the children's cleanliness (Chapter 15). She is in stark contrast to the parish nurse whom Lady Ashbrook had fired at the orphanage.

Another maternal figure is Aaron's foster mother, Mrs Camberwell, who is described as having 'thrown her apron over her head and howled' in grief at losing Aaron. Another kind-hearted but younger character is Mercy Bligh, the blind girl who comforts and advises Aaron and Toby.

## Key Quotations to Learn

… such intelligence, such a snake-like ability to target a person's weaknesses. (Mrs Peebles: Chapter 2)

An upright lady in a stiff bonnet and stiffly starched grey skirts … (Mrs Milcote: Chapter 4)

'Do not disgrace the Coram name. Do not let down the fine hopes your unknown mother had for you, nor the man who has succoured and ensured your well-being all this time.' (Mrs Hendry to Aaron and Toby: Chapter 19)

## Summary

- Mrs Milcote is starchy in character and concerned about appearances.
- Mrs Milcote refuses to talk to Melissa about the baby, but eventually shows regret before dropping down dead.
- Mrs Peebles and Mrs Lynch are manipulative characters involved in illegal and immoral trade. Mrs Lynch gives Melissa's baby to Otis.
- More kindly female figures include foster mother Mrs Camberwell, housekeeper Mrs Hendry and Mercy Bligh.

## Sample Analysis

Mrs Lynch is manipulative, scheming and unscrupulous. She is first described as dressing and using rouge in 'an effort to knock a decade off her age', indicating her deceptive nature. Her unkindness is shown by her pushing Meshak away and 'sharply' calling him 'an insolent pup'. At Mrs Milcote's funeral Melissa notices 'her eyes glittering – like a snake'. The **simile** makes her sound cold-hearted, treacherous and dangerous, and as if she looks forward to blackmailing Melissa.

## Questions

QUICK TEST
1. Why is Mrs Milcote at Ashbrook?
2. In what way does Mrs Milcote refuse to help Melissa?
3. Why does Mrs Peebles prefer the shadows?
4. Who is Coram's housekeeper?

EXAM PRACTICE
Write one or two paragraphs comparing your impressions of Mrs Hendry and Mrs Lynch.

**You must be able to:** understand how Gavin explores the themes of friendship and loyalty.

## What is the basis of the friendship between Alexander and Thomas?

Alexander and Thomas are thrown together at the choir school. When Thomas arrives, Alexander is given the job of 'showing him the ropes'. He is distant, and fails to protect Thomas from bullying, but instead tells him how to save himself by making the boys laugh. Strangely, Alexander still meets Thomas's jokes with 'a blank uncomprehending stare', but they bond when Thomas helps Alexander with algebra, and Alexander reciprocates with languages.

Their friendship is based on the attraction of opposites – Alexander so serious and Thomas light-hearted and outgoing. However, they are similar in that neither is pretentious, and both are kind-hearted.

Alexander has no social qualms about taking Thomas to Ashbrook and introducing him as his 'dearest friend'. Thomas engineers the reconciliation between Alexander and his family. However, the greatest act of loyalty comes when he takes the thrust of Gaddarn's sword and saves Alexander.

## Why are there ups and downs for Isobel and Melissa?

Isobel and Melissa become friends by default – they are the only teenage girls at Ashbrook, but their friendship is also based on their being opposites. Melissa has been brought up by a stiff and emotionally withdrawn mother, and is herself shy; Isobel is passionate, for example embracing Alexander 'fiercely' even after being told off by Mrs Milcote (Chapter 5).

Unlike the friendship between Alexander and Thomas, that between Isobel and Melissa has ups and downs, which relate to Melissa falling in love, starting her periods and becoming pregnant. She expects Isobel to spurn her when she reveals that she is pregnant, but Isobel proves a true friend.

## How is Aaron's loyalty to Toby challenged?

Aaron and Toby face similar challenges. In their first adventure, Aaron is prepared to face Mother Catbrain alone, whereas Toby insists that they should 'go together or stay together' (Chapter 15). Later, Aaron is reluctant to run away with Toby because he wants to become a musician. However, he shows loyalty when, without hesitation, he jumps overboard after Toby.

## Why is Meshak's loyalty complicated?

Meshak devotes himself to 'his angel' Melissa in Chapter 7, and he indirectly saves her from drowning. He also takes her baby to Coram instead of murdering it. He then transfers his loyalty to Aaron and, by association, Toby.

However, Meshak's loyalty is compromised by possessiveness when he fears that Aaron will be reclaimed (Chapter 29), and even more so when he knocks Alexander unconscious rather than let him take Aaron.

## Key Quotations to Learn

Where was Alexander, his supposed protector? he wondered bitterly. (Thomas: Chapter 4)

It was a long, long embrace of ... great comfort, friendship and love. (Isobel and Melissa: Chapter 13)

'He's not your son, he's my angel,' howled Meshak. 'Mine!' (Chapter 31)

## Summary

- Thomas and Alexander are unlikely friends. Thomas humanises Alexander and is loyal to him to the end.
- Isobel is passionate, Melissa shy. Their friendship wavers when Melissa falls in love and becomes withdrawn, and when she becomes pregnant, but it survives.
- Aaron and Toby are good friends, though Aaron is reluctant to run away with Thomas.
- Meshak is loyal to Melissa, then Aaron and Toby, but his possessiveness puts Aaron at risk.

## Sample Analysis

After Melissa has confessed to Isobel, the pair are 'together, always together; whispering, laughing, withdrawing into a private, secret world'. The repetition of 'together' adds emphasis and strengthens the sense of their excluding others. 'Whispering', 'withdrawing', 'excluding' and 'secret' all reinforce this, and create a sense of unreality: the girls are in denial, believing they can bring up a baby together. Isobel is loyal but encourages Melissa to deny reality: in the eighteenth century single mothers faced moral condemnation.

## Questions

QUICK TEST
1. How do Alexander and Thomas bond?
2. What happens that causes conflict in Isobel and Melissa's friendship?
3. Why does Aaron's passion for music make his loyalty waver?
4. How does Aaron show loyalty to Toby?
5. How does Meshak endanger Aaron?

EXAM PRACTICE
'In *Coram Boy* loyalty is more important in friendship than similarities.' Make a plan for an essay arguing for or against this statement.

# Love

**You must be able to:** understand how Gavin explores the theme of love.

## How do Alexander and Melissa fall in love?

The first indication of Alexander's attraction to Melissa is when he comments that she is 'quite amiable' (Chapter 7). In the same chapter he hears her playing the virginals and breaks into 'appreciative clapping', then asks 'admiringly' when she learnt. Given his love of music, this moment is significant.

It is unsurprising when, in Chapter 9, their playing music together leads to them kissing, witnessed by a horrified Meshak: 'Kissing. Mouth on mouth. Arms, cheeks, hair, neck.'

In Chapter 10 the relationship is developing: Isobel worries that Melissa may have taken her place as Alexander's closest friend, but also that Melissa may have 'quarrelled' with him. Melissa reassures her, falling just short of admitting that they are in love.

When Alice asks, 'Can Melissa marry Alex, then?' Melissa's blushing shows her embarrassment at hearing something that she may wish for herself.

## How do Alexander and Melissa come to make love?

In Chapter 12 Alexander is spending miserable days touring the estate, banned from playing music. Hence, when Melissa visits his bedroom, ostensibly just to suggest that he could play the cottage virginals, he finds 'his pent-up misery giving way to the sweetness of having Melissa in his arms'.

However, his first thought is to get dressed and go to play the instrument at Waterside. It is some time later, when he has resolved to leave Ashbrook, that she joins him while he is playing a particularly haunting piece of music, 'Dido's Farewell', by Purcell, in which a legendary queen of Carthage sings a **lament** before taking her own life because she has been abandoned by her lover. This is ironically appropriate, as Alexander is about to abandon Melissa.

She joins him singing and soon they are in each other's arms. His final word to her in the morning is 'Farewell'.

## Is Meshak in love with Melissa?

Meshak could be said to fall in love with Melissa, thinking she is 'his angel', but there never seems to be anything sexual in his feelings for her. Nonetheless he emits a 'wretched, wrenching howl' of jealous anguish when he sees her kissing Alexander. Later he transfers his love and loyalty to Aaron.

## How is non-romantic love shown in the novel?

There is, of course, **platonic love** within the novel's friendships. Isobel and Melissa feel love as friends, as do Alexander and Thomas – though nothing suggests that Alexander regrets losing Thomas when he leaves Ashbrook. Nonetheless, their close friendship is renewed when they meet again nine years later.

## Key Quotations to Learn

… her eyes gleamed, overflowing with happiness, and then their arms were round each other and they were kissing. (Melissa and Alexander: Chapter 9)

Melissa … turned a beetroot red then fled into the kitchen. (Chapter 10)

They lay in each other's arms all through the rest of the night, not knowing where affection ended and passion began. (Melissa and Alexander: Chapter 12)

## Summary

- Alexander and Melissa admire each other's musical ability, then fall in love.
- Isobel and Melissa's friendship is temporarily compromised by Melissa falling in love.
- Melissa visits Alexander in bed, but they only kiss and embrace.
- Alexander and Melissa make love the night before he leaves Ashbrook.
- Meshak adores Melissa, but transfers his loyalty to her son.

## Sample Analysis

It is a highly charged moment when Melissa joins in as Alexander is playing 'Dido's Farewell'. The way in which her voice simply comes in at the right moment to sing 'Remember me' shows how in tune they are emotionally. The simile 'like a dream' suggests that this moment is wonderful, but also that their union is unreal because they are so young and Alexander is about to leave.

## Questions

QUICK TEST
1. What adjective does Alexander first use to describe Melissa?
2. Why does Melissa feel sorry for Alexander?
3. What piece of music do Alexander and Melissa play together before he leaves?
4. What sight makes Meshak howl in distress?
5. To whom does Meshak transfer his love and loyalty?

EXAM PRACTICE
'In Coram Boy, friendship is more important than romantic love.' Write a plan for an essay arguing for or against this statement.

# Parenting

**You must be able to:** understand how Gavin explores the different styles of parenting.

## How is bad parenting shown?

It is hard to imagine how Otis could be a worse parent, even by harsh eighteenth-century standards. He regards Meshak as a burden, constantly abuses, bullies and beats him and neglects him for days on end. Worse, he forces him to 'get rid' of babies. Meshak is forever tormented by his memories. When, as a childlike adult, he seeks help from his father, Otis/Gaddarn kicks him in the head and ships him to America.

The stubborn and authoritarian Sir William at least has a sense of parental responsibility. He is not neglectful like Otis, but he lacks the imagination to understand his son's passion for music, and in fact despises it. The best that can be said for him is that he has allowed Alexander four years in the choir school, and thinks he will 'make a man of him' by forcing him to abandon music.

Mrs Milcote also has parental failings. She provides materially for Melissa, but she is an inflexible, emotionally remote mother concerned largely with class status and what is 'fit for young ladies' (Chapter 5). She does what she thinks best for Melissa, telling her that her baby is dead, but this lie is hard for both Melissa and the reader to forgive.

## How is good parenting shown?

The nearest Otis gets to good parenting is when he orders food and drink for Meshak. Sir William shows a better side as a parent when he shows remorse after nine years. Alexander unknowingly starts to become a good parent to Aaron as his music teacher.

Lady Ashbrook is a loving mother – Alexander is 'her adored son, on whose behalf she had argued and fought, to protect him from his stern and conscientious father' (Chapter 6). However, she eventually betrays him by siding with her husband.

The best example of parenting is presented by the Coram Hospital, which looks after its children in an enlightened way. It fosters the infant Aaron out to the kindly Mrs Camberwell, who calls him 'my dearest sweet boy, my baby' (Chapter 16). At Coram, Mrs Hendry personifies conscientious care. Her kindness is shown when she gives Aaron and Toby their mothers' keepsakes, 'kissing each boy on the top of the head' (Chapter 19).

## How are the difficulties of parenting in the eighteenth century shown?

The greatest difficulty of parenthood specific to the period context is illegitimacy, seen as a sin and 'an abomination' (Admiral Bailey: Chapter 6). This is why Melissa can't simply bring up her child, and why other mothers hand their babies over to Coram. However, another difficulty touched on in the novel is poverty.

## Key Quotations to Learn

Alexander was, as usual, giving her cause for concern. It was this wretched music. (Lady Ashbrook: Chapter 6)

He knew he was not the son his father hoped he would be. (Alexander: Chapter 8)

'And your da is meant to protect you, isn't he, angel? Just as I protect you?' (Meshak to Aaron: Chapter 31)

## Summary

- Otis is an abusive father who almost murders his own son.
- Sir William is stern and incapable of understanding or valuing Alexander's ability.
- Mrs Milcote is emotionally distant, though she tries to do the best for Melissa.
- The Coram Hospital represents good parenting.
- In the novel, illegitimacy is seen as a sin and a disgrace.

## Sample Analysis

Gavin shows that Lady Ashbrook is a loving mother, but she is exasperated by Alexander's desire to continue with music. She refers to it as 'this wretched music. Really! It was so ungentlemanly.' The adjective 'wretched' indicates her irritation and her value judgement, while the exclamation suggests both her annoyance and her belief that most people would agree. The word 'ungentlemanly' shows a typical class prejudice for the period.

## Questions

QUICK TEST
1. How has Otis/Gaddarn always regarded Meshak?
2. How has Alexander caused conflict between his parents?
3. How does Alexander begin to show that he will make a good father?
4. How is Mrs Hendry relevant to the theme of parenting?
5. Which character calls illegitimacy 'an abomination'?

EXAM PRACTICE
Write one or two paragraphs on how different aspects of parenting are contrasted in the novel.

# Charity and Exploitation

**You must be able to:** understand how charity and exploitation feature in the novel.

## What is the relationship between charity and exploitation?

Otis cynically says the Coram Hospital is funded by 'Money coming from the wealthy to salve their consciences and purchase their respectability' (Chapter 2). There could be some truth in this: some slave traders, such as Edward Colston of Bristol (died 1721), were also philanthropists. Gaddarn's dealing in black slaves would to most people at the time not seem at odds with his being a Coram benefactor.

Otis abuses charity by murdering babies he is paid to take to Coram. Admiral Bailey, who sits on the orphanage committee, is charged with conspiring with him to rid Ashbrook parish of the poor (Chapter 24). As Gaddarn, however, Otis takes hypocrisy to a new level. He enjoys a reputation as a donor to Coram, but he sells some of its children into slavery.

## Who behaves charitably in the novel?

Lady Ashbrook becomes involved with the orphanage and the poor after she and a friend find an abandoned child. When they visit the orphanage to enquire about her, they find that she died, and that the orphanage is a squalid place where children are starved and neglected. Lady Ashbrook has the woman in charge replaced and forms a committee to oversee the orphanage.

Lady Ashbrook clashes with committee members who are 'convinced that the better the conditions, the more it attracted children born out of wedlock – "an abomination", as she was sure Admiral Bailey would announce yet again.'

It could also be said that other characters behave charitably when they act generously. For example, the 'motherly' Mrs Morris advises Thomas on what to wear at Ashbrook.

## How is the Coram Hospital presented?

In the novel, the Coram children are treated kindly, and not exploited – except by Gaddarn. Mrs Hendry also represents Coram's benevolence, bustling 'like a mother hen' to make sure the children are clean and presentable. They are well cared for by 'the steward, the matron, governors, clerks and the apothecary, nurses, the schoolmaster and schoolmistress, cooks and cleaners' (Chapter 15).

At the same time the charity comes with value judgements and conditions. The children sing hymns that are 'supposed to remind them that they were all foundling children – abandoned, born out of shame', whose words are 'full of reproof and condemnation'.

## How is exploitation presented?

The prime exploiter is Otis/Gaddarn, but the farmers and mill owners to whom he sells children also exploit them. Even worse is seen in the slave trade, whose cruelty is presented through whips and chains, and through the slaves 'crammed, side by side, some barely living'.

## Key Quotations to Learn

Somehow, no matter what they did, the poor never seemed to get fewer. (Chapter 6)

They were never to forget that they bore the sins of their iniquitous mothers and fathers. (Coram children: Chapter 15)

It was as though they had been forgotten or didn't exist; nobody cared. (Slaves: Chapter 31)

## Summary

- Otis says the wealthy support the Coram Hospital out of guilt.
- Otis/Gaddarn exploits his role as a Coram benefactor.
- Lady Ashbrook works to improve the orphanage.
- The Coram Hospital is well-organised and caring but teaches the children that they are inferior.
- There are glimpses of the slave trade. Some slavers supported charities.

## Sample Analysis

The suffering of the slaves is vividly portrayed by Gavin through the senses of Aaron, Toby and Meshak. The **onomatopoeia** in 'the slash of the whips, the clank of chains' makes the cruelty more immediate, but the slaves' abject misery is conveyed by 'the long, low, endless moaning, like a wind which never ceased'. The sense of it going on without relief is heightened by the repetition and **alliteration**, and by the simile focusing on a ceaseless natural sound.

## Questions

QUICK TEST

1. Why is there no apparent conflict between Gaddarn supporting Coram yet being a slave trader?
2. What are Admiral Bailey's views on illegitimacy?
3. How is Thomas treated charitably at Ashbrook?
4. What shows that moral judgements are made on the Coram children?
5. Who oversees the welfare of the Coram children?

EXAM PRACTICE

Write one or two paragraphs on how characters behave charitably and exploitatively in the novel.

# Inspiration and the Arts

**You must be able to:** understand how Gavin explores the theme of inspiration and the arts.

## How is the passion for music represented?

Gavin is a classically trained musician, so she would have a clear insight into the character of Alexander, who, even at the age of 14, knows that he 'cannot live without music' (Chapter 12). The cathedral choir sings 'with piercing sweetness', but Alexander's voice soars above the others, 'causing a shiver of wonder at its purity'. However, Alexander does not just want to sing or enjoy music – he needs to compose in order to express the music inside him.

Thomas is also musical, but in a more light-hearted way. He loves to entertain, and he makes choir practices a pleasure for the Coram boys, but he lacks Alexander's serious passion, and is not a composer. Isobel, too, enjoys music, but Melissa has more talent, which Alexander appreciates.

Through Alexander, Gavin presents artistic creativity as essential to a higher level of human life. This is something that Sir William cannot begin to understand. He represents the attitude that holds only material things and money to be important – a view encapsulated in his comment on Alexander's compositions: 'Yes, yes, very nice but it won't bring in the harvest.'

Lady Ashbrook is more sympathetic, and Alexander has 'inherited her love of music' (Chapter 8). However, even she comes to condemn his passion for 'this wretched music' as 'ungentlemanly'. It seems that only Melissa really understands Alexander's attitude.

## How is music important at Coram?

Music offers the Coram children an experience of beauty that rises above the humdrum daily existence, even though some of the hymns they sing have words 'full of reproof and condemnation' for the parents who have abandoned them, and by association for the children themselves. It is the Coram Hospital that first nurtures Aaron's love of music.

The school is fortunate to have the great composer, George Frideric Handel, as a benefactor. Some of the children sing in the **debut** performance of his now-famous *Messiah*. This is a large-scale musical composition for orchestra, choir and soloists. Like much serious music of the time, its inspiration is Christian, and its words are taken from the Bible.

## What inspires Meshak?

While Meshak has no musical talent, he loves to hear the Gloucester Cathedral choir. His own life is physically and emotionally hard, so there is an element of escapism in his love of this music, and especially of the cathedral's angels. When he is 'dead' an angel takes him to another world where he can 'see' his dead mother. The angels created by medieval artists inspire him to experience a 'higher' and more fulfilling world.

## Key Quotations to Learn

He loved churches because there were angels there, sometimes within gleaming stained-glass windows or out in the graveyards; stone angels with gentle hands and loving faces. (Meshak: Chapter 1)

… the overwhelming need for music – as great a need as a starving man has for food. (Alexander: Chapter 12)

What Aaron loved most in this strict, solemn hospital school was the music. (Chapter 15)

## Summary

- Alexander represents the need for artistic creativity.
- Thomas loves music, but lacks Alexander's passion for it.
- Sir William cannot understand anyone needing to be a musician.
- The composer Handel is a benefactor of the Coram Hospital.
- Meshak escapes into a higher consciousness inspired by the cathedral's angels.

## Sample Analysis

We see the importance of musical inspiration in the performance of Handel's *Messiah*. First, there is its physicality: 'the vibrations of the strings, and the bassoons shivering through his bones, and the plucked beat of the harpsichord and the rattle of the timpani'. The verb 'shivering' conveys the thrill of excitement that Aaron feels in the core of his being. The words 'vibrations', 'plucked' and 'rattle' express the unique character of each instrument.

## Questions

QUICK TEST
1. From whom does Alexander inherit a love of music?
2. What is the inspiration for Handel's *Messiah*?
3. Who dismisses music as serving no practical purpose?
4. Who is a talented entertainer but not a composer?
5. What art inspires Meshak?

EXAM PRACTICE
Write a paragraph on the importance of music in *Coram Boy*.

**You must be able to:** understand how to approach the exam question and meet the requirements of the mark scheme.

## Quick Tips

- You will get a choice of two questions, each based on a short quotation from the novel. One is likely to be on a character, the other on a theme. You will be told to refer to the context of the novel in your answer.
- The question will carry 40 marks, including 8 marks for using a range of appropriate vocabulary and sentence structures, with accurate spelling and punctuation.
- Make sure you know what the question is asking you. Underline key words. Consider how the question might be interpreted. For example, if you are asked about courage in the novel, think of the many ways in which a character can show courage.
- You should spend about 50 minutes on your *Coram Boy* response. Allow yourself between five and ten minutes to plan a well-structured answer.
- It can sometimes help, after each paragraph, to quickly reread the question to keep yourself focused on the exam task.
- Keep your writing concise. If you waste time 'waffling', you won't be able to include the breadth and depth of ideas that the mark scheme requires.
- Refer to the context of the novel, but don't write a long account of it. Keep what you say strictly relevant to elements of the plot, characters or themes.
- It is a good idea to remember what the mark scheme is asking of you.

## AO1: Understand and respond to the novel (16 marks)

This is all about coming up with a range of points that match the question, interpreting and explaining Gavin's ideas, supporting these ideas with references from the novel, and writing your essay in a mature, academic style.

| Lower | Middle | Upper |
|---|---|---|
| The essay has some good ideas that are mostly relevant. Some quotations and references are used to support the ideas. | A clear essay that always focuses on the exam question. Quotations and references support ideas effectively. The response refers to different points in the novel. | A convincing, well-structured essay that answers the question fully. Quotations and references are well-chosen and integrated into sentences. The response covers the whole novel (not everything, but ideas from a range of chapters). |

# AO3: Understand the relationship between the novel and its contexts (16 marks)

For this part of the mark scheme, you need to show your understanding of how the characters, plot or Gavin's ideas relate to the period when the novel is set (1741–50) relative to the present day.

| Lower | Middle | Upper |
|---|---|---|
| Some awareness of how ideas in the novel link to its context. | References to relevant aspects of context show a clear understanding. | Exploration is linked to specific aspects of the novel's contexts to show a detailed understanding. Context is fully integrated. |

# AO4: Use a range of vocabulary and sentence structures for clarity, purpose and effect, with accurate spelling and punctuation (8 marks)

You need to use a range of accurate vocabulary, punctuation and spelling in order to convey your ideas clearly and effectively.

| Lower | Middle | Upper |
|---|---|---|
| Reasonable level of accuracy. Errors do not get in the way of the essay making sense. | Good level of accuracy. Vocabulary and sentences help to keep ideas clear. | Consistently high level of accuracy. Vocabulary and sentences are used to make ideas clear and precise. |

# Practice Questions

1. *From now on, he would be her guardian and protector.*
   In what ways is Meshak important in the novel?
   You **must** refer to the context of the novel in your answer.

2. *... the shadow of Otis Gardiner still lingered and encircled the world like a menacing whirlwind ...*
   Explore the significance of Otis in *Coram Boy*.
   You **must** refer to the context of the novel in your answer.

3. *'Without music I cannot be a man.'*
   In what ways is Alexander important in the novel?
   You **must** refer to the context of the novel in your answer.

4. *They lay in each other's arms all through the rest of the night.*
   Explore the relationship between Alexander and Melissa.
   You **must** refer to the context of the novel in your answer.

5. *Thomas threw himself over his friend. Without even a cry, he took the brunt of the murderous thrust.*
   Explore the relationship between Thomas and Alexander.
   You **must** refer to the context of the novel in your answer.

6. *Toby liked Mr Ledbury. Everyone did. He was young and funny and often made them laugh when he taught them hymns.*
   In what ways is Thomas important in the novel?
   You **must** refer to the context of the novel in your answer.

7. *'We must make amends and try to save other children from that hell.'*
   What is Lady Ashbrook's significance in the novel?
   You **must** refer to the context of the novel in your answer.

8. *... their father could be so stern and demanding and critical of his son.*
   How is Sir William important in the novel?
   You **must** refer to the context of the novel in your answer.

9. *'Melissa is my dearest friend – my sister,' enthused Isobel, throwing an arm round her shoulders.*
   Explore the relationship between Isobel and Melissa.
   You **must** refer to the context of the novel in your answer.

10. *'You must not encourage or sympathise with your brother's selfishness.'* (Lady Ashbrook)
    What is Isobel's significance in the novel?
    You **must** refer to the context of the novel in your answer.

11. *... he wanted to be a musician more than anything else in the world.*
    How is Aaron important in the novel?
    You **must** refer to the context of the novel in your answer.

12. *He would be given a silver platter laden with sweetmeats which he had to hand round to all the guests.*
    Explore Toby's importance in the novel.
    You **must** refer to the context of the novel in your answer.

13. *An upright lady in a stiff bonnet and stiffly starched grey skirts …*
    How is Mrs Milcote important in the novel?
    You **must** refer to the context of the novel in your answer.

14. *Melissa wondered if Mrs Lynch thought she could transfer that power to enthrall her.*
    How is Mrs Lynch significant in the novel?
    You **must** refer to the context of the novel in your answer.

15. *'All of our children are foundling children; children who were found by the wayside or in porches and doorways.' (Mrs Hendry)*
    How is the Coram Hospital important in the novel?
    You **must** refer to the context of the novel in your answer.

16. *No bird sang sweeter, no friend was truer, no man was ever more missed.* (Thomas's epitaph)
    Explore the importance of friendships in the novel.
    You **must** refer to the context of the novel in your answer.

17. *It was a long, long embrace of such great comfort, friendship and love …* (Isobel and Melissa)
    Explore the different ways in which love is important in the novel.
    You **must** refer to the context of the novel in your answer.

18. *'And your da is meant to protect you, isn't he, angel? Just as I protect you?' (Meshak)*
    Explore how parenting is important in the novel.
    You **must** refer to the context of the novel in your answer.

19. *Somehow, no matter what they did, the poor never seemed to get fewer.*
    In what ways is charity significant in the novel?
    You **must** refer to the context of the novel in your answer.

20. *They were a cargo of slaves who had just come in from Africa and who were to be put on board a slave ship bound for the West Indies.*
    Explore how exploitation is shown to be important in the novel.
    You **must** refer to the context of the novel in your answer.

21. *Aaron sang as he had never sung before and, suddenly, he knew again that there was nothing else in life that he wanted to be except a musician.*
    Explore the importance of music in the novel.
    You **must** refer to the context of the novel in your answer.

# Planning a Character Question Response

**You must be able to:** understand what an exam question is asking you and prepare your response.

## How might an exam question on character be phrased?

A typical character question will read like this:

*From now on, he would be her guardian and protector.*

In what ways is Meshak important in the novel?

You **must** refer to the context of the novel in your answer.

[40 marks] (includes 8 marks for the range of appropriate vocabulary and sentence structures, and accurate use of spelling and punctuation)

## How do I work out what to do?

The focus of this question is clear: Meshak and his importance in the novel.

'Ways', 'important' and 'context' are the key elements of this question.

For AO1, these words show that you need to display a clear understanding of what Meshak is like and how this relates to the themes of the novel and Gavin's intentions.

For AO3, you need to link your interpretations to the novel's social, historical or literary context.

You also need to remember to write in an accurate and sophisticated way to achieve your 8 AO4 marks for spelling, punctuation, grammar and expression.

## How can I plan my essay?

You have approximately 50 minutes to write your essay.

This isn't long but you should spend the first five or ten minutes writing a quick plan. This will help you to focus your thoughts and produce a well-structured essay.

Try to come up with four or five ideas. Each of these ideas can then be written up as a paragraph.

You can plan in whatever way you find most useful. Some students like to just make a quick list of points and then re-number them in a logical order. Spider diagrams are particularly popular; look at the example on the opposite page. Note that this is much fuller than you would have time for in your five-minute plan.

Gains sympathy from start: only 14, abused and exploited by Otis, and has fits. Remains childlike. Bad parenting. Pathetic that he hopes Otis/Gaddarn will help; instead kicks and ships him to America.
*'Oi! Meshak! Wake up, you lazy dolt!'*
*'I have a da. And your da is meant to protect you, isn't he, angel? Just as I protect you?'*

Pivotal to plot: kills babies for Otis, becomes obsessed with Melissa and so saves Aaron. Takes him to Coram. Later abducts him from Ashbrook. Aaron almost lost. Knocks out Alexander; Thomas dies.
*From now on, he would be her guardian and protector.*
*With one swinging blow across the head with his giant hand, he knocked Alexander unconscious to the ground.*

## Ways Meshak is important

Embodies one type of artistic inspiration: adores cathedral angels. 'His' angel shows him his dead mother. Is he deluded or a mystic? His obsession with Melissa is touching but dangerous.
*His brain filled with images; dreams overwhelmed him.*

Gothic figure like Mary Shelley's creature in *Frankenstein*. A lonely, monstrous, misunderstood outsider longingly peering through windows. Ambiguous: kind to Aaron and Toby, but kills babies, abducts Aaron and tries to keep him from parents.
*Someone stood on the lawn outside, staring at an upstairs window of the house; a raggle-taggle fellow. ... Thomas shuddered. Filled with unease, he closed the shutters.*

Epilogue narrated from Meshak's viewpoint, portraying him late in life. Gives sense of completion.
*'Can I be dead now?'* he asked her. *'Is it time?'* *'Yes,'* she smiled. *'Yes, yes, yes. It is time.'*

## Summary

- Make sure you know what the focus of the essay is.
- Remember to interpret the character: what do they represent and what ideas are being conveyed?
- Try to relate your ideas to the novel's context and Gavin's intentions.

## Questions

QUICK TEST
1. What key skills do you need to show in your answer?
2. What are the benefits of quickly planning your essay?
3. Why do you need to take care with your writing?

EXAM PRACTICE
Plan a response to the following exam question.
*'Fool of a boy. Why was I so cursed with a son like you?'*
Explore the relationship between Meshak and Otis/Gaddarn.
You **must** refer to the context of the novel in your answer.

*From now on, he would be her guardian and protector.*

In what ways is Meshak important in the novel?

You **must** refer to the context of the novel in your answer.

[40 marks] (includes 8 marks for the range of appropriate vocabulary and sentence structures, and accurate use of spelling and punctuation)

*Meshak is a rather mixed character. He deserves the reader's sympathy because he is so badly treated by his cruel father Otis, but he also poses a threat to other characters (1).*

*Gavin demonstrates Otis's cruelty right at the start. 'Oi! Meshak! Wake up, you lazy dolt!' Children in the eighteenth century were mostly not treated well, but Meshak's father uses a whip on him just to wake him up, and gives him all the dirty work of killing the babies. When Meshak has his fits and becomes 'dead', Otis tries to beat him out of it until Mrs Peebles tells him they are fits and to leave him to get over them. There was not much understanding of this kind of illness then (2).*

*Amazingly, nine years later Meshak still hopes that his father will help him out after he has run off with Aaron. He tells Aaron: 'I have a da. And your da is meant to protect you, isn't he, angel? Just as I protect you?' We see he is basically kind but he is like a child, too optimistic and trusting (3).*

*Meshak is important in the story because he gets fixed on Melissa being 'his angel' from Gloucester Cathedral and spies on her all the time. He decides to become 'her guardian and protector'. He does actually save her at one point just by being by the pond when she is about to drown herself. She thinks he is the devil (4).*

*When Otis hands him her baby to get rid of, instead he takes Aaron to the Coram Hospital where he is safe. On the other hand, when Meshak worries that Melissa has recognised Aaron, he kidnaps him and takes him into danger. As a result he almost gets sent as a slave to America. 'He knocked Alexander unconscious to the ground.' There was still a slave trade in London at that time (5).*

*It is hard to say if Meshak has special religious visions when the angel takes him to see his dead mother, and when he sees the babies' ghosts. He could just be mad (6). He is big and ugly, and has no friends his own age, so he is a bit of a loner. He also seems quite threatening the way he keeps spying on Melissa and howls like a wolf 'a sound so raw and harsh' when she kisses Alexander (7).*

*Gavin makes Meshak's importance clear at the end. The Epilogue is told from his point of view as an old man. He has had a lot of adventures in America but we never get told about them, just that no one really believes him when he talks about them. It is very touching and gives a feeling of completion when he asks his angel at the end if he can 'be dead now' and she smiles and says he can (8).*

*Without Meshak there would really be no plot. It is appropriate that the book begins and ends with him. He also makes the novel more interesting by adding danger and the unexpected due to his unpredictable behaviour (9). Lastly, he shows that even someone like him can play an important role in life and achieve things that affect other people (10).*

1. A basic and simple introduction which highlights contrasting aspects of Meshak but that would benefit from more specific details about theme and intention. AO1

2. Develops the introduction and uses textual evidence, though it could be better integrated and analysed more. Some appropriate context, but it is not well integrated. Some language ('dirty work') too informal. AO1/AO3

3. Makes a simple but effective interpretation of textual evidence. AO1

4. Uses embedded quotations but does not analyse their significance. Makes an interesting point but it needs to be explained more fully. AO1

5. Effectively highlights the contradiction in Meshak's character, but expression could be clearer and more sophisticated. The quotation could be embedded and its significance explained. The contextual point is accurate but a little 'bolted on'. AO1/AO3

6. Points out an important question of interpretation in the character, though the expression could be more sophisticated. AO1

7. Uses evidence quite well, but expression ('a bit of') could be more sophisticated. Quotation is fairly well embedded. AO1
Could have earned marks for AO3 by relating this to the Gothic genre.

8. Shows an awareness of structure and shows an informed personal response. Some phrasing is rather vague.

9. Attempts an assessment of the character's importance in the novel as a whole. AO1

10. An acceptable but slightly vague conclusion. AO1

> ## Questions
>
> EXAM PRACTICE
> Choose a paragraph from this essay. Read it through a few times then try to rewrite and improve it. You might:
> - Improve the sophistication of the language or the clarity of expression.
> - Replace or supplement a reference with a quotation.
> - Ensure quotations are embedded in the sentence.
> - Provide a clearer interpretation of Meshak's character.
> - Provide more context and link it to the interpretation more effectively.

# Grade 7+ Annotated Response

A proportion of the best top-band answers will be awarded Grade 8 or Grade 9. To achieve this, you should aim for a sophisticated, fluent and nuanced response that displays flair and originality.

*From now on, he would be her guardian and protector.*

In what ways is Meshak important in the novel?

You **must** refer to the context of the novel in your answer.

[40 marks] (includes 8 marks for the range of appropriate vocabulary and sentence structures, and accurate use of spelling and punctuation)

*Meshak is an important character for Gavin in several ways. By having him earn the reader's sympathy for the abusive way in which he is treated, she highlights the evil behaviour of Otis/ Gaddarn. He is also a complex character through whom the author explores the relationship between mystical experience and mental illness. Finally, he is central to plot development because of his impetuous actions in first taking baby Aaron to Coram, and then kidnapping him eight years later (1).*

*The novel begins with a whole paragraph of Meshak being abused: 'Oi! Meshak! Wake up, you lazy dolt!' Far from appreciating or encouraging him, Otis belittles him and sees him as a burden: 'Fool of a boy. Why was I so cursed with a son like you?' Even by the standards of the eighteenth century this is harsh (2). In response, the poor boy stumbles around trying to please his father and avoid a beating. It is extraordinary that nine years later he still naively thinks his father might help him with Aaron. He tells Aaron, 'I have a da. And your da is meant to protect you, isn't he, angel?' Even when his furious father 'lashes out' and kicks Meshak in the head, his pathetic response is to apologise for running away eight years earlier (3).*

*Despite being abused, Meshak remains sensitive and compassionate. He hates burying dead or nearly dead babies in ditches, as ordered by Otis – it gives him 'frightful nightmares' – and he is kind and protective to Aaron and Toby. He could be seen as a replacement father to them, in keeping with the novel's parenting theme (4).*

*Nonetheless he is an ambiguous character. His lack of understanding, coupled with his 'giant' size and strength, make him a threat. He places Aaron in danger when he kidnaps him and takes him to Gaddarn. Worse, when Alexander and Thomas come to the rescue, Meshak's possessiveness makes him attack Aaron's real father, knocking Alexander unconscious 'with one swinging blow across the head with his giant hand'. As a result, Thomas dies saving his defenceless friend from Gaddarn (5).*

*This ambiguity links Meshak to the Gothic genre popular in the early nineteenth century, but still effective in modern times when the novel was written (6). Meshak is misunderstood: 'People assumed that he was nothing but an empty vessel,' but this is untrue. He has a sensitive though simple-minded appreciation of the cathedral's angels and music, and his adoration of Melissa, then Aaron, shows his capacity for love (7). His resolution to become her 'guardian and protector' shows his good intentions. However, his obsessive stalking of her, and his animal howling when she kisses Alexander, make him seem threateningly unpredictable. He becomes like the monstrous 'creature' in Mary Shelley's 'Frankenstein'. Even when he saves Melissa by being at the pond in which she intends to drown herself, she sees him not as a saviour but as the 'devil ... watching me' – a sad misunderstanding, given his devotion to her (8).*

*Appropriately for the genre, it is on a windy moonlit night that Thomas sees him 'staring at an upstairs window of the house' and is 'filled with unease'. This could be seen as foreshadowing or even a premonition, since Meshak eventually causes his death (9).*

*The Epilogue, narrated from Meshak's viewpoint, underlines how important he is. Indeed, the author was at one point going to begin with this chapter and tell the whole story as a flashback (10). However, finishing the novel with Meshak's poignant question to 'his angel', 'Can I be dead now?' and her replying 'Yes, yes, yes. It is time', gives a satisfying sense of completion. The reader can feel sympathy as he goes to meet the mother he has always longed for (11).*

1. Well-structured introduction beginning with topic sentence and outlining three points developed later. AO1

2. Good use of textual evidence; integrated historical context. AO1/AO3

3. Embedded textual evidence and personal response. AO1

4. Textual evidence; personal interpretation. AO1

5. Effective paragraph beginning with topic sentence and developing essay's argument. Embedded quotation as evidence. AO1

6. Demonstrates awareness of literary context and time of writing. AO3

7. Effective personal interpretation with sophisticated expression. AO1/AO4

8. Develops ideas about Gothic genre, with further personal response. AO3/AO1

9. Develops genre point; effective point about literary technique, with correct term. AO3/AO1

10. Interesting contextual information integrated into argument. AO3/AO1

11. Effective conclusion with personal response. AO1

## Questions

EXAM PRACTICE

Spend 50 minutes writing an answer to the following question:

*'Fool of a boy. Why was I so cursed with a son like you?'*

Explore the relationship between Meshak and Otis/Gaddarn. You **must** refer to the context of the novel in your answer. [40 marks, including 8 AO4 marks]

Remember to use the plan you have already prepared.

# Planning a Theme Question Response

**You must be able to:** understand what an exam question is asking you and prepare your response.

## How might an exam question on a theme be phrased?

A typical theme question will read like this:

*No bird sang sweeter, no friend was truer, no man was ever more missed.* (Thomas's epitaph)

Explore the importance of friendships in the novel.

You **must** refer to the context of the novel in your answer.

[40 marks] (includes 8 marks for the range of appropriate vocabulary and sentence structures, and accurate use of spelling and punctuation)

## How do I work out what to do?

The focus of this question is clear: the way friendships feature in the novel.

'Explore', 'importance' and 'context' are the key elements of this question.

For AO1, these words show that you need to display a clear understanding of what friendships there are in the novel and how these relate to the themes of the novel and Gavin's intentions.

For AO3, you need to link your interpretations to the novel's social, historical or literary context.

You also need to remember to write in an accurate and sophisticated way to achieve your 8 AO4 marks for spelling, punctuation, grammar and expression.

## How can I plan my essay?

You have approximately 50 minutes to write your essay.

This isn't long but you should spend the first five or ten minutes writing a quick plan. This will help you to focus your thoughts and produce a well-structured essay.

Try to come up with five or six ideas. Each of these ideas can then be written up as a paragraph.

You can plan in whatever way you find most useful. Some students like to just make a quick list of points and then re-number them in a logical order. Spider diagrams are particularly popular; look at the example on the opposite page. Note that this is much fuller than you would have time for in your five-minute plan.

Friendships reveal and develop the characters. Gavin reveals characters through how they form friendships and how they treat their friends. Characters develop as personalities through the challenges that friendships bring and through threatened and actual losses. *'This fellow, John, is my dearest friend, so I hope you'll look out for him ...'* *'You could have stopped him. You've ruined our lives.'*

First friendship introduced is Alexander and Thomas. Initially mutual interest – they help each other with schoolwork. Then opposites attract. Alexander serious and introverted; Thomas light-hearted extrovert. Loyal friends despite class differences. Thomas gives life to save Alexander. *'If you can make them laugh, they'll never trouble you again.'* *... when he saw Alexander drifting helplessly over a calculation, he offered to help him.*

**Importance of friendships**

Next friendship is Isobel and Melissa. At first based on lack of other opportunities, but then they complement each other. Isobel passionate, impulsive; Melissa shy, sensitive. Their friendship is challenged by Melissa falling in love with Alexander, then getting pregnant. The friendship is strengthened by the pregnancy, but then it fades out of the narrative. *It was a long, long embrace of such great comfort, friendship and love ...*

Thomas makes the ultimate sacrifice, bringing tragedy to the end of the story. Grieved by Alexander. Might give message that friendship is most important thing in life. *... no man was ever more missed.*

Aaron and Toby are firm friends. Aaron is bolder and more independent. They plan to run away together, but Aaron's passion for music intervenes. But it is Toby who saves Aaron by escaping Gaddarn and fetching help. Shows the role of loyalty and courage echoed by Alexander and Thomas. Aaron loyal when Toby jumps into sea. *'I ain't not leaving you. We go together or stay together.'* *Aaron didn't think or cry out ... he just tipped himself over the side.*

## Summary

- Make sure you know what the focus of the essay is.
- Remember to interpret the theme. How is it shown? What ideas are conveyed?
- Try to relate your ideas to the novel's context and Gavin's intentions.

## Questions

QUICK TEST
1. What key skills do you need to show in your answer?
2. What are the benefits of quickly planning your essay?
3. Why do you need to take care with your writing?

EXAM PRACTICE
Plan a response to the following exam question.
*'... allow me to be of help in advising you what to wear.'* (Mrs Morris to Thomas)
Explore the importance of charity in *Coram Boy*.
You **must** refer to the context of the novel in your answer.

# Grade 5 Annotated Response

*No bird sang sweeter, no friend was truer, no man was ever more missed.* (Thomas's epitaph)

Explore the importance of friendships in the novel.

You **must** refer to the context of the novel in your answer.

[40 marks] (includes 8 marks for the range of appropriate vocabulary and sentence structures, and accurate use of spelling and punctuation)

*There are three main friendships – Alexander and Thomas, Isobel and Melissa, and Aaron and Toby. The author uses them to show us what the characters are like, and how they change as the novel goes on. All these friendships meet challenges, and the characters respond in various ways (1).*

*The first friendship is Alexander and Thomas. Gavin shows this beginning in a very low-key way. Alexander has to show Thomas around at school, but Thomas gets bullied anyway, as all new boys were in those days (2), until Alexander cleverly tells him how to stop it: 'If you can make them laugh, they'll never trouble you again.' This shows that even though Alexander is very serious he has noticed Thomas is an entertainer (3).*

*After this they become friends because Thomas is good at algebra. He notices Alexander stuck on a sum: 'Alexander drifting helplessly over a calculation.' (4) Alexander accepts his help. The boys are from different classes, Alexander upper class and Thomas the son of 'a ship's carpenter'. In those days class was an important divider (5). Despite this they become best friends, so Alexander invites Thomas to his home. Alexander says 'This fellow, John, is my dearest friend, so I hope you'll look out for him and show him the ropes if he seems lost.' This shows he can be a warm and caring friend (6).*

*Thomas is at first put off by Alexander's huge house and servants, but he stays friends with him. He entertains Alexander and the others and becomes popular. Alexander's mother Lady Ashbrook thanks Thomas for 'turning him into a human being'. This shows they are good for each other (7).*

*Isobel and Melissa is another main relationship. They are the only teenagers at Ashbrook, but also they do get along well. Gavin presents them as another 'opposites attract' case. Isobel is passionate and rushes into things, and Melissa is shy. 'Oh, you are a silly thing. Why be shy in front of Thomas?' Also Melissa has a very uptight mother (8). The two fall out because Melissa falls for Alexander and Isobel gets jealous, but they iron this out. Then Isobel is frustrated because she knows something is wrong with Melissa. But when Melissa confesses she is pregnant, to her surprise Isobel hugs her. 'A long, long embrace of such great comfort, friendship and love' (9). This is a relief to Melissa because at that time a teenage pregnancy was shameful and usually kept secret (10).*

*The big friendship in Part 2 is Aaron and Toby. Possibly Jamila wanted to show that black and white could be friends, even then. They have adventures, like when they taunt Mother Catbrain, but Aaron is bolder. He tells Toby he can run away if he wants. Toby shows loyalty by saying 'I ain't not leaving you. We go together or stay together.' He is also loyal when he tries to save Aaron by escaping Gaddarn's house and fetching help. Aaron shows he is loyal too by jumping into the sea after Toby. Earlier he let Toby down by not running away with him because he wanted to be a musician (11).*

*However, the biggest example of friendship is when Thomas saves Alexander from Gaddarn's sword and dies himself. This shows how important loyalty is in friendship, then and now. All three pairs of friends are loyal to each other despite the challenges they face (12).*

1. Accurate but mechanical and simplistic introduction listing friendships. Could instead structure essay by dealing with different aspects of friendship, comparing all three. AO1

2. Integrated but rather simplistic context. AO3

3. Explains significance of quotation simply but quite effectively. AO1

4. Appropriate quotation but could easily have been embedded in sentence. AO1

5. Context but simplistic and 'bolted on' rather than integrated. AO3

6. Good deduction but the way it is presented ('This shows that ...') becomes repetitive. AO1

7. Another good deduction repetitively presented. AO1

8. Some unsophisticated and overly informal language. AO4

9. Accurate, but begins to simply retell the story. AO1

10. A relevant contextual point but too simplified and unintegrated. AO3

11. Some good points that could be more fluently expressed and more effectively ordered. AO1

12. A moderately effective conclusion attempting a simple synthesis of ideas. AO1

## Questions

Choose a paragraph from this essay. Read it through a few times then try to rewrite and improve it. You might:

- Improve the sophistication of the language or the clarity of expression.
- Replace or supplement a reference with a quotation.
- Ensure quotations are embedded in the sentence.
- Provide an interpretation showing how Gavin presents differences and similarities in the friendships.
- Provide more context and link it to the interpretation more effectively.

A proportion of the best top-band answers will be awarded Grade 8 or Grade 9. To achieve this, you should aim for a sophisticated, fluent and nuanced response that displays flair and originality.

*No bird sang sweeter, no friend was truer, no man was ever more missed.* (Thomas's epitaph)

Explore the importance of friendships in the novel.

You **must** refer to the context of the novel in your answer.

[40 marks] (includes 8 marks for the range of appropriate vocabulary and sentence structures, and accurate use of spelling and punctuation)

*Gavin uses friendships to reveal characters in depth and to develop them through the challenges they face. She seems particularly interested in how opposites attract. She also explores issues of loyalty versus individual needs (1).*

*Opposites certainly attract for Alexander and Thomas. Thomas is outgoing, as is shown when he offers to help Alexander when he is 'drifting helplessly over a calculation' in algebra, and the introverted Alexander 'grudgingly' accepts. Alexander reciprocates with languages. Then, when Thomas proves to be a 'skilful performer' on the violin, Alexander writes music for him. These beginnings show how the boys complement each other, despite their differences: 'No two boys were more unlike each other: Alexander introverted and gloomy, Thomas popular and sociable.' Their personalities contrast, but Thomas appreciates Alexander's musicality and in his company Alexander becomes, as Lady Ashbrook puts it, 'a human being' (2).*

*Opposites also attract in the novel's other friendships. Gavin creates an impression of Isobel as impulsive and passionate, 'flying' to greet Alexander, and 'burbling' in excitement. We see the same warmth when she introduces Melissa as 'my dearest friend – my sister'. Melissa, brought up by a 'stiff' mother who holds herself 'so proudly', is more withdrawn. We see how Isobel helps to bring her out of herself: 'Oh, you are a silly thing. Why be shy in front of Thomas?' (3)*

*In the case of Aaron and Toby there is the superficial contrast in skin colour that makes people call them 'Night and Day', and which would have seemed remarkable in the eighteenth century, but also in Aaron being 'the bolder' of the two, as we see when they taunt Mother Catbrain. A further difference emerges when Aaron realises that he wants 'to be a musician more than anything else in the world'. Toby's greatest wishes are to be free from Gaddarn and to find his mother (4).*

*Gavin also explores class differences in the relationships that at the time would have mattered more than now. Alexander is a 'gentleman' living in 'the finest house Thomas could ever have imagined', while Thomas is the son of 'a ship's carpenter' whose sister goes barefoot. Although Thomas initially struggles at Ashbrook, class never divides them. Alexander still introduces Thomas as 'the most splendid fellow that ever walked the earth' (5).*

With Isobel and Melissa the class difference is slight by modern standards, but still significant for the period, as Melissa's widowed mother has been obliged to become Ashbrook's governess. There is no suggestion of Isobel looking down on her for this. Melissa, however, risks becoming a social outcast when she becomes pregnant out of wedlock. Yet, despite her fear of condemnation, when she confesses, she and Isobel share 'a long, long embrace of ... great comfort, friendship and love', showing that friendship can overcome social prejudice (6).

Melissa's pregnancy in fact bonds them more closely, 'always together; whispering, laughing, withdrawing into a private, secret world', as they naively plan to raise the baby. In the case of Aaron and Toby, the challenge is Aaron's musical ambition, which stops him from 'running away' with Toby. Yet he shows impulsive loyalty when he 'tips himself over the side' of a ship to follow Toby (7).

Alexander and Thomas's friendship is challenged by Alexander leaving Ashbrook. Nonetheless the pair resume it as if uninterrupted nine years later, Aaron noticing how they 'become like boys again' when together. Tragically, in the novel's climax (8), Thomas shows his utter loyalty to Alexander by taking 'the brunt' of Gaddarn's 'murderous thrust'. This noble, unthinking loyalty is echoed later when Aaron follows Toby overboard (9).

Overall Gavin shows that friendships can develop despite differences of class, colour or temperament, and can survive challenges, providing the friends find a balance between individual need, as in Alexander and Aaron's music, and loyalty (10).

1. Concise introduction interprets author's intentions and relates question to theme. AO1
2. Explores theme using embedded quotations. A well-structured paragraph with a variety of sentence types and sophisticated punctuation. AO1/AO4
3. Explores the same aspect – opposites attracting – in another friendship. AO1
4. Develops the argument with a third friendship, integrating historical context. AO1/AO3
5. Introduces another challenge to friendship, relating it to historical context; well-chosen embedded quotations. AO1/AO3
6. Develops idea of class differences, with well-integrated context, making an important point. A fluent paragraph using connectives (e.g. 'however') and sophisticated punctuation. AO1/AO3/AO4
7. Effective comparison; embedded quotations. AO1
8. Awareness of structure; appropriate use of terms. AO1/AO4
9. Effectively compares friendships. AO1
10. Effective conclusion synthesising ideas rather than just repeating them. AO1

### Questions

EXAM PRACTICE
Spend 50 minutes writing an answer to the following question:
'... allow me to be of help in advising you what to wear.' (Mrs Morris to Thomas)
Explore the importance of charity in *Coram Boy*. You **must** refer to the context of the novel in your answer. [40 marks, including 8 AO4 marks]
Remember to use the plan you have already prepared.

# Glossary

**Alliteration** – repetition of sounds, especially at the beginning of words, for effect; e.g. 'long, low'.

**Ambiguous** – open to more than one interpretation (noun 'ambiguity').

**Antagonist** – character directly opposed to or threatening a main character – in *Coram Boy* this is Otis/Gaddarn.

**Aristocratic** – relating to, or coming from, a family that has been wealthy and powerful for many generations, often since the Norman Conquest (1066).

**Benefactor** – someone who gives financial support to a charity.

**Climax** – the most important and exciting part of a novel, usually near the end – in *Coram Boy* the tragic death of Thomas.

**Crisis** – in a novel, the point of highest danger, when key characters have the most to gain or lose – in *Coram Boy* the point when Alexander confronts Gaddarn; may coincide with the *climax* or come just before it.

**Debut** – the first ever performance of a piece of music or a play; also used to describe a first novel.

**Epilogue** – a chapter or section at the end of a novel or play, giving it a conclusion and a sense of completion.

**Falling action** – the final part of a novel coming after the *climax*, in which tension relaxes and loose ends are tied up.

**Fate** – the idea that events turn out in a predetermined way.

**Flashback** – a device in which the story is told in retrospect, looking back in time from its starting point.

**Foreshadowing** – literary technique in which a story hints at events yet to come.

**Genre** – a particular type of novel, play, film, etc., with recognisable characteristics; e.g. *Gothic*

**Gothic** – relating to a literary *genre* featuring horror, death, gloomy or dramatic scenes, nightmares and misunderstood or monstrous individuals.

**Illegitimacy** – the state of a child born to unmarried parents.

**Industrial Revolution** – period roughly 1760–1840 when machine production of goods in factories was getting underway, fuelled by coal and the manufacture of metals, and supplied by raw materials from British colonies like the West Indies.

**Irony** – something that seems the opposite of what was expected; deliberately using words that mean the opposite of what is intended.

**Lament** – sad song expressing regret or loss.

**Mystic** – one who pursues or perceives spiritual truths that are beyond ordinary perception of the material world.

**Narrative** – story, or relating to a story.

**Onomatopoeia** – the use of words that sound like what they signify; e.g. 'clank'.

**Parish** – a small, defined country area that has its own church, vicar and council to make decisions about local matters.

**Platonic love** – intimate but non-sexual love between friends.

**Protagonist** – the leading character in a novel, usually the one the reader is encouraged to empathise with the most.

**Simile** – an image creating a word picture by comparing something to another thing that it resembles in some way; e.g. Mrs Lynch's eyes glitter 'like a snake'.

**Social mobility** – the movement of people, through acquiring wealth, from their original social class to a higher one.

**Supernatural** – that which cannot be explained by scientific materialism, such as ghosts or magic.

**Tragic** – relating to tragedy, an artistic *genre* involving the death of a noble hero or heroine through *fate* or a character flaw.

**Triangular trade** – trade shipping British goods to Africa, slaves to the West Indies and America, and raw materials (especially sugar and cotton) back to Britain.

**Virginals** – a musical instrument with a keyboard which is used to pluck strings.

**Ward** – a young person under the guardianship of someone other than their parents.

**Welfare state** – collection of modern government institutions aiming to prevent extreme poverty and foster the health and welfare of the population.

# Answers

## Pages 4–5

### Quick Test

1. He gets Meshak to bury them in a ditch by the road.
2. He loves the angels in the stained glass and stone monuments. He also enjoys hearing the choir.
3. Mrs Lynch
4. He entertains the boys and makes them laugh.
5. She is stiff and stand-offish – disdainful.

### Exam Practice

Answers might include: Otis behaves abusively towards Meshak, verbally abusing him as an 'idiot', frequently beating him, and using a whip just to wake him up or make him move faster – as if he is an animal. At other times he simply neglects him. He resents Meshak as a burden rather than appreciating him. Meshak puts up with this silently and without complaint.

## Pages 6–7

### Quick Test

1. She offers to advise him on what to wear.
2. He thinks they should turn more mothers and children away from the orphanage, and that improving conditions will encourage illegitimacy.
3. Waterside – the 'play cottage'.
4. Mrs Lynch
5. He sees Melissa and Alexander kissing.

### Exam Practice

Answers might include: Sir William does not understand Alexander's passion for music. Alexander and Melissa are falling in love. Their parents may object to this, partly because they are so young. The class difference between Alexander and Thomas could be a problem. There could be ongoing clashes between Lady Ashbrook and Admiral Bailey over funding of the orphanage.

## Pages 8–9

### Quick Test

1. This foreshadows Melissa becoming pregnant by Alexander.
2. Alexander's voice breaks.
3. Melissa and his father
4. Mrs Lynch arranges to get rid of Melissa's baby in secret.
5. Meshak. He takes it to the Coram Hospital.

### Exam Practice

Answers might include: It means he is taken away from the choir school and has to give up music and start learning estate management. This makes him decide to leave Ashbrook. It also makes Melissa sympathetic towards him, deepening her feelings for him. It makes her remind him that he could still play the virginals at Waterside. When he does, she joins him and they make love, which leads to her pregnancy.

## Pages 10–11

### Quick Test

1. She can turn into a cat.
2. Handel/Mr Burney
3. Handel hears Aaron sing and suggests that he could be apprenticed to Mr Burney.
4. America
5. The mementoes (keepsakes) left with them by their mothers.

### Exam Practice

Answers might include: Aaron and Toby share an adventure as friends, with Aaron being bolder and Toby being more loyal. Their friendship is challenged by Aaron's passion for music: he wants to stay in London and become a musician, not run away with Toby. Old friends Alexander and Thomas are delighted to meet again after nine years.

## Pages 12–13

### Quick Test

1. 'The Silver Swan'
2. Alexander is hired as musical director at one of Gaddarn's parties.
3. Toby has escaped a party by going to a side room (the map room), where he falls asleep. He is awoken by Gaddarn discussing business with his associates.
4. A performance of Handel's *Messiah*.
5. Thomas believes that Otis was hanged. In fact Otis managed to make it widely believed that it was he who had been hanged, when in fact it was someone else.

### Exam Practice

Answers might include: The first hint of Otis/Gaddarn being exposed is when Alexander, musical director at one of his parties, thinks he has seen him before. At the performance of Handel's *Messiah* he realises that Gaddarn is Otis. Toby overhears Gaddarn discussing his illegal business, and knows he must tell someone in order to prevent it.

## Pages 14–15

### Quick Test

1. Melissa
2. He feels guilty about keeping Aaron from Melissa.
3. He has forgiven Alexander and wants him to become part of the family again.
4. She is running after Meshak, demanding to know 'what happened to the child'.
5. He fears losing Aaron because Melissa is realising that Aaron is her child.

### Exam Practice

Answers might include: Melissa wants to move on from her past, and has begun to mistrust Mrs Lynch, who had previously appeared to be her helper. She and her mother have found a new purpose in life at the orphanage. Mrs Milcote finally confesses the truth about the baby. Meshak is experiencing a moral challenge over keeping Aaron from Melissa, making him speak harshly to Aaron for the first time. Sir William admits to regret over how he treated Alexander.

**Pages 16–17**

Quick Test

1. A portrait of Alexander as a boy.
2. Toby tells them.
3. Meshak
4. Gaddarn
5. He is about to jump overboard when a sailor 'swipes' him off the side of the ship.

Exam Practice

Answers might include: Toby is brave to escape from Gaddarn's house to fetch help to save Aaron and Meshak. Aaron is brave to jump overboard. Alexander and Thomas are both brave to confront Gaddarn, especially as he is protected by a crew of sailors. Thomas is extremely courageous to throw himself over Alexander's body to protect him from Gaddarn's sword.

The conniving and manipulative Mrs Lynch is preparing to blackmail Melissa, as she previously blackmailed Mrs Milcote. However, Gaddarn is arguably more villainous, having made a fortune by selling into slavery the children he is supposed to help as a benefactor of the Coram Hospital. He is prepared to do anything to retain his lifestyle, including murdering Alexander – although it is actually Thomas he kills.

**Pages 18–19**

Quick Test

1. Nine
2. He forces Alexander to leave the choir school.
3. It begins with Aaron and Toby as happy Coram boys. At this point they have no particular problems.
4. He saves Aaron as a baby, and he kidnaps him and takes him to London when he thinks that Melissa may be realising who he is.
5. Meshak

Exam Practice

Answers might include: Alexander being forced to leave choir school; Alexander making love with Melissa, then leaving Ashbrook; Melissa having her baby, and it being saved by Meshak; Alexander recognising Gaddarn as Otis; Toby discovering Gaddarn's child-trafficking business; Alexander and Thomas confronting Gaddarn; Toby being knocked overboard and Aaron following him.

**Pages 20–21**

Quick Test

1. The ferry to cross the Severn at Framilode.
2. Robbers and highwaymen
3. Ashbrook
4. Gaddarn stabs Thomas.
5. Bloomsbury – then just outside London.

Exam Practice

Answers might include: The Black Dog inn is a lively, and rather seedy, drinking place frequented by sailors, where the barmaids expect heavy-handed flirting from the clientele, and whose owner, Mrs Peebles, negotiates deals involving disposing of illegitimate babies. Ashbrook is a large estate, with extensive land, a beautiful house and gardens, and many servants. It is occupied by the wealthy aristocratic Ashbrook family.

**Pages 22–23**

Quick Test

1. He inherited it.
2. Coming from a wealthy family, far from giving him freedom, actually prevents him from doing what he most wants.
3. From being a pedlar, Otis has been able to build up his wealth, investing money in various enterprises, including slavery, to the point where he lives like a gentleman and is able to host extravagant parties.
4. Governess, housekeeper, barmaid, nurse.
5. They died.

Exam Practice

Answers might include: There is financial inequality between Alexander and Thomas; Alexander lives in a mansion on an estate, with servants, while Thomas lives in a tiny house shared by his large family. More broadly, the poor are present in the novel in Lady Ashbrook's involvement in the orphanage and the poor of her parish generally. Conditions at the orphanage are squalid. Even the charitable Coram Hospital sets out to preserve inequality by making sure the children feel inferior to those born in wedlock and not abandoned by their parents.

**Pages 24–25**

Quick Test

1. Sugar
2. Cotton
3. By drowning in the sea.
4. He has seen how many rich people love to have a black child servant because they seem exotic.
5. London, Bristol and Liverpool

Exam Practice

Answers might include: His mother has been shipped to America as a slave. He lives under threat of being sent to America as a slave himself if he displeases Gaddarn. Even if he becomes a servant in another household he may be treated as little better than a slave.

**Pages 26–27**

Quick Test

1. Carrying out and/or funding charitable works to benefit the less fortunate, theoretically out of love for humanity.
2. Christianity
3. 'General Reception' (1756–60), when it was paid by the state to admit all babies.
4. Admiral Bailey
5. Mementoes – keepsakes

Exam Practice

Answers might include: It was founded by retired sea captain Thomas Coram, who persuaded a lot of wealthy people to fund it. Illegitimate babies were taken there, fostered out, then taken back there aged about five. Children were cared for until they could be found work or apprenticeships. Mothers often left mementoes with their babies, and the Hospital took great care of these. Some 'Coram men' did earn money during the period of 'General Reception' by taking illegitimate babies there.

# Answers

## Pages 28–29
### Quick Test
1. Horror, death, the supernatural, nightmares, social misfits, romance
2. He is a lonely, misunderstood social misfit who spies on the happiness of others.
3. Those of the babies he has been made to bury in ditches.
4. She sees Meshak's reflection and thinks it is the devil come to fetch her.
5. No one knows how he has become wealthy or where he comes from.

### Exam Practice
Answers might include: Meshak sees the ghosts of babies. When he has fits he meets 'his angel', who takes him to see his dead mother. He speaks to her at the end of the novel, when he can finally meet his mother. Mother Catbrain accurately reads Aaron's palm, telling him that he is a gentleman.

## Pages 30–31
### Quick Test
1. He is tall and gangly, with an overly large head of wild red hair, a pale freckled face, watery blue eyes, and a mouth hanging open and drooling.
2. He hates having to bury them.
3. He thinks Gaddarn/Otis will help him keep Aaron.
4. He is a lonely, strange-looking and misunderstood individual who deserves sympathy but becomes a threat because of his obsessive love.
5. America

### Exam Practice
Answers might include: He is important in deserving our sympathy and highlighting how cruel and immoral Otis/Gaddarn is. He raises questions about the relationship between mysticism and mental illness. He is pivotal to the plot because he saves Melissa's baby, kidnaps Aaron eight years later and knocks Alexander unconscious, which leads to Thomas's death.

## Pages 32–33
### Quick Test
1. Alexander
2. He makes the young mother think he will treat her baby with great care, and tells Meshak to do the same.
3. He somehow arranges for another criminal to be hanged in his place, so people think he is dead.
4. He thinks they give money because they have guilty consciences.
5. Nothing – as far as we know, he remains free.

### Exam Practice
Answers might include: Gaddarn is widely respected as a generous donor to the Coram Hospital, and for arranging work for some of its children when they are old enough to leave it. In reality, his contributions are a front. He enjoys his reputation. In addition he sells children to become slaves or to join harems. He employs Toby, but treats him cruelly and speaks of selling him into slavery.

## Pages 34–35
### Quick Test
1. Alexander gets the job of showing Thomas how the choir school works; then they help each other in lessons.
2. He becomes best friends with Thomas, son of a carpenter.
3. He says she is 'quite amiable'.
4. It turns out that he wrote her letters, which were intercepted.
5. He offers to speak up for him and get him transported instead of being hanged.

### Exam Practice
Answers might include: He has a passion for music. He is kind to Thomas and to his siblings. He tells Thomas how to stop being bullied. He tries to obey his father's wishes for the sake of the family. He falls in love with Melissa and writes her letters. He confronts Gaddarn. On the other hand, he deserts Melissa the morning after having sex with her. He also deserts his family.

## Pages 36–37
### Quick Test
1. He is a ship's carpenter.
2. He makes them laugh and entertains them.
3. He blames his own horsemanship.
4. He makes the Coram boys laugh when he teaches them hymns.
5. He throws himself over the unconscious Alexander, bearing the brunt of Gaddarn's sword thrust.

### Exam Practice
Answers might include: Thomas is perceptive and sensitive, and has a keen sense of humour. He can tell stories, like that of Dawdley Dan, and entertain musically. He is also self-effacing, for example, blaming himself when he falls from a horse. He is also a loyal friend.

## Pages 38–39
### Quick Test
1. She and a friend visit the orphanage to check on an abandoned child they found and discover the appalling conditions there.
2. She has the parish nurse sacked and replaced, raises money to fund it and forms a committee to run it.
3. He furiously challenges his father.
4. She sides with Sir William in ruling that Alexander must now leave choir school and learn to manage the estate.
5. He disinherits him.

### Exam Practice
Answers might include: She takes care of the abandoned girl. She feels responsibility for the poor living on Ashbrook land and in her parish. She works to improve conditions at the orphanage by replacing the parish nurse, raising money and forming a management committee.

## Pages 40–41
### Quick Test
1. Melissa's mother becomes governess at Ashbrook. Then Isobel and Melissa develop a relationship intensified by there being no other teenage girls there.
2. Isobel is impulsive and passionate; Melissa is more cautious and shy.
3. She thinks Melissa has taken her place as Alexander's friend and confidante.
4. Alexander leaving Ashbrook.

Exam Practice

Answers might include: We see more emotional development in their friendship than in that of Alexander and Thomas. Their embracing in love and understanding, after Melissa confesses her pregnancy, is a very moving moment. Melissa is central to the plot in that she falls in love with Alexander, and is Aaron's mother. It is also Melissa who makes the connection between the visiting Aaron and the portrait of Alexander as a boy.

## Pages 42–43

Quick Test

1. Aaron
2. To find his mother.
3. He wants to stay in London and become a musician.
4. He overhears Gaddarn discussing how he sells them to become slaves or join harems.
5. To avoid becoming a slave.

Exam Practice

Answers might include: He is bold. He has a great passion and talent for music. In particular he sings beautifully, as his father did before his voice broke. He has a best friend.

## Pages 44–45

Quick Test

1. She is widowed and needs work, so becomes governess to the Ashbrook children.
2. She refuses to talk about the lost baby, so Melissa cannot properly grieve.
3. She is pock-marked from smallpox.
4. Mrs Hendry

Exam Practice

Answers might include: Mrs Hendry seems firm but kind, making sure the children are clean. Aaron and Toby worry about her telling them off, but they do not fear her. She treats them kindly when she gives them their mothers' mementoes. Mrs Lynch is manipulative, dressing and wearing make-up to look younger, and flirting with Otis to persuade him to do business with her. She is a hard-hearted woman who is willing to give Melissa's baby to Otis knowing it will probably not survive.

## Pages 46–47

Quick Test

1. They help each other with school work.
2. Melissa falls in love with Alexander and becomes pregnant by him.
3. He wants to stay in London and become a musician rather than run away with Toby.
4. He jumps overboard when a sailor pushes Toby into the sea.
5. He kidnaps Aaron and takes him to Gaddarn in London.

Exam Practice

Answers might include: Alexander and Thomas are very different – Alexander serious and introverted, and Thomas outgoing and light-hearted, and their class backgrounds differ, but they do have music in common, and a basic kindness. Alexander shows loyalty when he risks unpopularity by helping Thomas avoid bullying. Thomas is very loyal in laying down his life for Alexander. Isobel and Melissa are different in character but have love for Alexander in common. Isobel is loyal to Melissa when she gets pregnant. Aaron and Toby have Coram and a love of adventure in common but are otherwise quite different. They both show loyalty to each other – Toby by running to fetch help to rescue Aaron, and Aaron by jumping overboard after Toby.

## Pages 48–49

Quick Test

1. Amiable
2. His father removes him from the choir school, removes all musical instruments from the house and makes him learn estate management.
3. 'Dido's Farewell', by Purcell. Also known as 'Dido's Lament'.
4. The sight of Melissa and Alexander kissing.
5. Aaron, and to some extent Toby.

Exam Practice

Answers might include: There are three strong friendships in the novel, and only one love affair. The friendships are all positive and supportive, despite the misunderstandings between Isobel and Melissa, whereas Alexander and Melissa's love causes distress – the unwanted pregnancy, grief over the supposedly lost child and Alexander abandoning Melissa. This grief is foreshadowed by Alexander and Melissa playing and singing 'Dido's Lament'. The description of Alexander and Melissa's night of love is intense, but then the moment is over. There is little space given to their reunion. On the other hand, Gavin develops the friendships in depth.

## Pages 50–51

Quick Test

1. As a useless burden.
2. By wanting to be a musician.
3. By being a good music teacher to Aaron.
4. Coram's housekeeper, she acts like a mother to the children there.
5. Admiral Bailey

Exam Practice

Answers might include: Otis is the worst possible parent – bullying, belittling and brutal. He refuses to help Meshak and ships him to America. Alexander and Melissa could be called bad parents in that they become parents unintentionally and their child is almost murdered, and is then brought up in an institution. Alexander unwittingly becomes a good parent figure to Aaron as his teacher. Sir William is a harsh and unsympathetic parent, though behaving in a way that was not unusual for an eighteenth-century aristocrat.

## Pages 52–53

Quick Test

1. Black slavery was widely accepted as morally permissible in eighteenth-century Britain.
2. He thinks it is morally unacceptable – 'an abomination'.
3. Mrs Morris offers to advise him on what to wear.
4. They are taught to sing hymns whose words embody the belief that being illegitimate and abandoned makes them inferior.
5. Mrs Hendry

Exam Practice

Answers might include: Lady Ashbrook and her friend are charitable in their treatment of an abandoned child they find, and in improving conditions at the orphanage. Lady Ashbrook battles against the uncharitable Admiral Bailey on the committee. Otis/Gaddarn is exploitative, selling children to mill owners and farmers, blackmailing young mothers and selling Coram children into slavery. The Coram Hospital is a charitable institution, and Mrs Hendry is a charitable individual working for it.

# Answers

## Pages 54–55

Quick Test

1. Lady Ashbrook
2. Christianity
3. Sir William
4. Thomas
5. Cathedral angels in stained-glass windows and stone monuments.

Exam Practice

Answers might include: Alexander is passionate about music, for which he is prepared to give up Melissa, his family and his inheritance of Ashbrook. He has difficult years in Europe but persists and by the second part of the novel is becoming known in London as a musician, and is even respected by Handel. Thomas enjoys music in a more light-hearted way. His making a career in music means that he does not have to become a carpenter. Melissa also loves music, and it helps to bring her and Alexander together.

## Pages 58–59

Practice Questions

Use the mark scheme at the end of the Answers section to self-assess your strengths and weaknesses. The grade descriptors are included to help you assess your progress towards your target grade.

## Pages 60–61

Quick Test

1. Understanding of the whole text, use of textual evidence, awareness of the relevance of context, a well-structured essay and accurate writing.
2. Planning focuses your thoughts and allows you to produce a well-structured essay.
3. There are 8 marks available for using a range of accurate vocabulary, punctuation and spelling in order to convey your ideas clearly and effectively.

Exam Practice

Answers might explore Otis's brutal and neglectful treatment of Meshak – he whips the boy, disparages him constantly (see opening), and leaves him to fend for himself for days – and his exploitation of him, making him bury babies (sometimes alive) in ditches. They could look at Meshak's unquestioning acceptance of this, his surprisingly rebellious flight with baby Aaron and his continued naive trust in Otis/Gaddarn. They might cite the context of poor treatment of children and adolescents in the eighteenth century, but emphasise that Otis is an abusive parent even by these standards – though he does stop short of killing Meshak.

## Pages 62–63

Sample Upgrade of Paragraph 1:

*Meshak is a key character in the narrative because so much of the plot stems from his becoming obsessed with Melissa. He thinks she is 'his angel' from the stained glass in Gloucester Cathedral, and therefore spies on her whenever he has the opportunity. This leads to him saving her baby, Aaron, and kidnapping him eight years later. His devoted nature is shown when he resolves to become Melissa's 'guardian and protector'. Ironically, when he does actually save her life, just by being at the pond when she is about to drown herself, it is because she thinks he is the devil.*

## Pages 64–65

Exam Practice

Use the mark scheme at the end of the Answers section to self-assess your strengths and weaknesses. Work up from the bottom, putting a tick by things you have fully accomplished, a ½ by skills that are in place but need securing, and underlining areas that need particular development. The estimated grade boundaries are included so you can assess your progress towards your target grade.

## Pages 66–67

Quick Test

1. Understanding of the whole text, use of textual evidence, awareness of the relevance of context, a well-structured essay and accurate writing.
2. Planning focuses your thoughts and allows you to produce a well-structured essay.
3. There are 8 marks available for using a range of accurate vocabulary, punctuation and spelling in order to convey your ideas clearly and effectively.

Exam Practice

Answers might explore charity on an individual and social level. Individually, some characters are charitable in that they are kind and/or generous to those who are less fortunate (for example, Mrs Morris to Thomas, as in the quotation; Alexander to Thomas; Handel to Aaron; Mrs Hendry to the Coram children; Lady Ashbrook to orphans). On a social level, Coram Hospital is funded by generous individuals. Answers might also explore the context of eighteenth-century motives for charity, such as Christian piety and the desire for reputation. (Gaddarn enjoys a charitable reputation but abuses his role.)

## Pages 68–69

Sample Upgrade of Paragraph 2:

*The first friendship Gavin introduces is that of Alexander and Thomas. This begins unpromisingly when Alexander has to show Thomas around as a new boy at school. Alexander seems indifferent to him, and initially fails to prevent him from being bullied – a common occurrence in eighteenth-century boarding schools. However, this changes when Alexander finds a way to tell Thomas that the boys will not 'trouble' him if he can 'make them laugh'. This reveals Alexander's compassion, his cleverness, and the fact that despite his introverted nature he appreciates Thomas's sense of humour and ability to entertain.*

## Pages 70–71

Exam Practice

Use the mark scheme at the end of the Answers section to self-assess your strengths and weaknesses. Work up from the bottom, putting a tick by things you have fully accomplished, a ½ by skills that are in place but need securing, and underlining areas that need particular development. The estimated grade boundaries are included so you can assess your progress towards your target grade.

| Grade | AO1 (16 marks) | AO3 (16 marks) | AO4 (8 marks) |
|---|---|---|---|
| 6–7+ | A convincing, well-structured essay that answers the question fully. Clear interpretation of a range of different aspects of the novel. Quotations and references are well chosen and integrated into sentences. The response covers the whole novel. | Exploration is linked to specific aspects of the novel's contexts to show a detailed understanding. Context is integrated with interpretation. | Consistently high level of accuracy. Vocabulary and sentences are used to make ideas clear and precise. |
| 4–5 | A clear essay that focuses on the exam question. Some interpretation of different aspects of the novel. Quotations and references support ideas effectively. The response refers to different points in the novel. | References to relevant aspects of context show a clear understanding. | Good level of accuracy. Vocabulary and sentences help to keep ideas clear. |
| 2–3 | The essay has some good ideas that are mostly relevant. There is an attempt to interpret a few aspects of the novel. Some quotations and references are used to support the ideas. | Some awareness of how ideas in the novel link to its context. | Reasonable level of accuracy. Errors do not get in the way of the essay making sense. |

# The Inspirations Behind *Coram Boy*

from Jamila Gavin

A chance remark here, a conversation there; these are the serendipitous encounters that can trigger a book.

The chance remark that gave birth to *Coram Boy* was hearing about a 'Coram Man' who trafficked children, perhaps in the eighteenth century. "Who or what was a Coram Man?" I had asked. But no one knew. It sounded like an urban myth. I went to the London telephone directory and looked up 'Coram'. There were only half a dozen, but after a couple of phone calls I got to what was then called the Coram Foundation. It was 'open sesame!' The Coram Hospital, as it was first called, had been founded in London by a certain Captain Coram in 1739. From impoverished cabin boy to wealthy ship owner, Captain Coram had become "fed up with tripping over the dead and dying bodies of abandoned babies" and decided to open a place of refuge for them – remembering that the original meaning of the word 'hospital' comes from a Latin root meaning 'friendliness to guests'. His inspiration led to the first Foundling Hospital for the *'Education and Maintenance for exposed and deserted young children'*.

Even the word 'foundling' was intriguing. What's the difference between a foundling and an orphan? The foundling was very likely illegitimate – therefore a product of sin, whereas an orphan has had two parents but with the misfortune that both had died. So, an orphan goes to an orphanage without stigma, unlike the foundling. Oliver Twist was a foundling.

The chance conversation came the following summer when I was tutoring for an Arvon course in Heptonstall, near Hebden Bridge in Yorkshire. One day, while walking, I stopped to chat with a local man and, as I was admiring the beautiful wooded slopes around us, he said, "We locals call them the 'Crying Woods'" because of all the poor children who were worked to death in the mills, and were buried roughly in the woods because their families couldn't afford proper funerals. Some people think they hear their cries.

Almost instantly, the whole scenario for a book leapt into my head. Almost fully clothed came my characters, the rich, the poor, the good, the evil.

As I tried to absorb myself into eighteenth-century England, I realised that my own experience of India was a good parallel. I had seen poverty among the pavement dwellers on the streets of Calcutta and Mumbai. I had seen how the rich skim over them – each knowing their own class, caste, or position – and accepting that's how things are. Surely, eighteenth-century London had been the same?

My greatest love in life had been music. I had loved playing the piano and composing. In reading as a child, I realised that despite being geniuses, and despite the awe and respect that they got in their lives, in class terms people like Bach, Handel, Mozart, Haydn and Beethoven were 'trade'. They never walked through the front doors of the palaces where they served, but by the tradesmen's entrances. I was finally understanding the intricacies of class division – and the way society worked. This interest was right at the heart of my inspiration for *Coram Boy*, and for the character Alexander. *Coram Boy* is really my own exploration of how society worked in those days: their attitudes, especially to the poor, and to children. Corruption and cruelty were not confined to class – but were accepted behaviour from the classrooms of Eton and the cathedral choir schools, to the streets of London.

Two things can cut across any class divide, and do so in *Coram Boy*: music and friendship.